ALGARVE TRAVEL GUIDE 2024

Delve into the Historical Sites, Beaches, Restaurants, Outdoor Activities and Accommodation options in Portugal's stunning Region

Emmaline Gill

All rights reserved. No part of this publication may be reproduced, distributed, or transmitted in any form or by any means, including photocopying, recording, or other electronic or mechanical methods, without the prior written permission of the publisher, except in the case of brief quotations embodied in critical reviews and certain other noncommercial uses permitted by copyright law.

Copyright © Emmaline Gill, 2024.

Table of Contents

INTRODUCTION 4
   A Personal Journey into Portugal's Coastal Paradise 4
   1.1 Overview of Algarve 6
   1.2 Best Time to Visit Algarve 13
   1.3 Getting to Algarve 22

CHAPTER 2: ALGARVE AT A GLANCE 28
   2.1 Geography and Climate 28
   2.2 Culture and History 33
   2.3 Local Cuisine 39

CHAPTER 3: PLANNING YOUR TRIP 46
   3.1 Visa and Entry Requirements 46
   3.2 Health and Safety 52
   3.3 Budgeting for Your Trip 56

CHAPTER 4: ACCOMMODATION 58
   4.1 Hotels and Resorts 58
   4.2 Vacation Rentals 63
   4.3 Camping and Caravanning 68

CHAPTER 5: TRANSPORTATION 76
   5.1 Getting Around Algarve 76
   5.2 Public Transportation 82
   5.3 Car Rentals 84

CHAPTER 6: ITINERARY 90
   6.1 Day 1: Arrival and Exploring Faro 90
   6.2 Day 2: Lagos and Ponta da Piedade 93
   6.3 Day 3: Silves and Monchique 96

- 6.4 Day 4: Tavira and Ria Formosa... 98
- 6.5 Day 5: Sagres and Cape St. Vincent..................................... 100
- 6.6 Day 6: Albufeira and Surroundings 103
- 6.7 Day 7: Departure or Optional Activities 106

CHAPTER 7: ATTRACTIONS AND ACTIVITIES......................... 108

- 7.1 Beaches.. 108
- 7.2 Historical Sites 115
- 7.3 Outdoor Activities 124
- 7.4 Nightlife 130

CHAPTER 8: FOOD AND DRINK 134

- 8.1 Traditional Dishes 134
- 8.2 Best Restaurants... 136
- 8.3 Local Markets.. 143

CHAPTER 9: SHOPPING 148

- 9.1 Souvenirs and Local Crafts 148
- 9.2 Shopping Centers and Outlets 151

CHAPTER 10: PRACTICAL INFORMATION 154

- 10.1 Currency and Payments 154
- 10.2 Local Customs and Etiquette... 156
- 10.3 Useful Phrases in Portuguese 158

CONCLUSION 162

Introduction

A Personal Journey into Portugal's Coastal Paradise

As I reminisce about my journey through the Algarve, I'm enveloped by the warmth of the golden sun and the gentle embrace of the Atlantic breeze. It was a travel experience transcending mere sightseeing and an intimate dance with the region's soul. My adventure began in the bustling streets of Faro, where the city's vibrant energy was a prelude to the serene beauty that lay ahead. Each step through the cobbled lanes was a step back in time, with the whispers of history echoing off ancient walls.

The Algarve's coastline, a masterpiece painted by nature's finest brush, was a revelation. The diversity was astounding, from the dramatic cliffs of Sagres, where the land boldly kisses the sea, to the tranquil waters of Tavira, where time seems to stand still. The beaches were not just stretches of sand but sanctuaries of peace, each with its own story to tell. The flavors of the Algarve linger on my palate like a sweet memory. The succulent seafood, the rich aroma of piri-piri, and the irresistible taste of pastéis de nata created a symphony of flavors that defined the essence of Portuguese cuisine.

The Algarve is more than just a destination; it's a vibrant tapestry woven with threads of culture, tradition, and modernity. Whether the soulful strains of Fado that filled the night air or the colorful festivals that celebrated the region's heritage, the Algarve's culture captivated my heart.

This travel guide is a culmination of all the wonders I've experienced, crafted to ensure your journey is as magical as mine. It's a companion that understands the traveler's heart, offering information and inspiration. Let this guide be your gateway to creating your own unforgettable Algarve story. In this guide, you'll find the landmarks, must-sees, and hidden nooks and crannies that often go unnoticed. It's a guide that speaks to the wanderer in search of authenticity, the dreamer yearning for beauty, and the adventurer eager for discovery. Join me as we explore the Algarve together through the eyes of someone captivated by its charm and eager to share it with you.

1.1 Overview of Algarve

Welcome to the Algarve, where the sun kisses the sea and the golden sands whisper tales of ancient mariners. This southernmost region of Portugal is not just a destination; the encounter unfolds like to a colorful tapestry adorned with cultural strands, nature, and gastronomy. Embarking on a journey to the Algarve is akin to opening a book filled with enchanting stories. Your narrative begins as you descend into Faro Airport, a modern facility that introduces you to this captivating region. Here, the balmy air greets you, hinting at the adventures ahead.

Getting There: Chart your course by renting a car upon arrival. This option offers the ultimate flexibility, allowing you to meander through the Algarve's scenic routes and hidden gems at your own pace. The airport has handy locations for car rental companies, providing a range of vehicles to suit your preferences and budget. If you prefer to lean back and watch the world go by, the Algarve's public transportation is at your service. Trains and buses run punctually, connecting Faro to alluring destinations like Lagos, Tavira, and Albufeira. The train offers a comfortable ride with the chance to gaze upon the rolling landscapes, while buses provide direct access to the heart of each town, often at a lower cost.

Navigating the Region: The Algarve's transportation network is designed for easy use, with clear signage and helpful staff ready to assist you. Whether you choose the independence of a car or the simplicity of public transit, you'll find the Algarve to be a region that's both accessible and welcoming.

As you set out from Faro, the roads unfurl like ribbons, leading you through olive groves, past whitewashed villages, and along the rugged coastline. Each mode of travel offers a unique perspective on this land of contrasts, where the bustle of beachside resorts exists in harmony with the tranquility of secluded coves. So, pack your bags, bring your sense of wonder, and prepare for an unforgettable voyage to the heart of Portugal's southern splendor. The Algarve is not just a place on the map; it's a destination etched in the soul, waiting to be explored and cherished.

In the Algarve, your accommodation is more than just a place to sleep—it's a part of your journey. The region offers a diverse array of lodgings that cater to every preference and budget, ensuring that your stay is as memorable as the landscapes you'll explore.

Accommodation Options:

Luxury Resorts: The Algarve's luxury resorts provide an oasis of comfort and elegance for those who desire the finer things in life. The AP Eva Senses in Faro is a prime example, offering guests a 4-star experience with its contemporary design, attentive service, and amenities, including a rooftop swimming pool where you can soak up the sun and take in the expansive waterfront vista. You'll be welcomed with a complementary breakfast every morning to make the most of the beginning of your day.

Boutique Hotels: If you're drawn to the unique and intimate, the boutique hotels throughout the region offer a personalized touch. These charming establishments often reflect the Algarve's rich cultural heritage in their architecture and decor, offering a comfortable haven after a day of discovery.

Budget-Friendly Stays: The Stay Hotel Faro Centro exemplifies the Algarve's commitment to accessibility. Located in the vibrant heart of Faro, this hotel is a stone's throw away from local attractions and dining options. It's ideal for travelers who prioritize convenience and value without sacrificing comfort.

Choosing Your Stay: When selecting your accommodation, think about how close it is to the locations you want to see. The Algarve is dotted with picturesque towns with its character and charm. Whether you stay in the bustling city of Faro, the historic streets of Silves, or the tranquil retreats near the Ria Formosa lagoon, there's a perfect spot for you. Remember, your choice of accommodation can enhance your experience. A room with a view might offer a glimpse of the fishing boats as they return with the day's catch, or a balcony might provide the perfect vantage point for the region's spectacular sunsets.

In the Algarve, every accommodation tells a story. Whether it's the whisper of the ocean breeze through your window or the warm hospitality of your hosts, you'll find that your chosen home away from home adds its chapter to the tale of your travels. As you travel through the Algarve, your palate will embark on a journey as rich and varied as the landscapes. Dining here is not just about sustenance; it's about stories, tradition, and celebrating local bounty.

Dining in the Algarve:

The Bold Octopus: Nestled on the edge of Quinta do Lago, The Bold Octopus is a culinary beacon for seafood lovers. Here, the day's catch is transformed into gastronomic artistry. Imagine savoring a plate of tender octopus, grilled to perfection and drizzled with local olive oil, as you gaze out over the lagoon's tranquil waters. The restaurant's commitment to freshness and quality is evident in every bite, and the panoramic views add a visual feast to the experience.

Local Traditions: The Algarve's culinary scene is deeply rooted in tradition, and there's no better place to experience this than at the annual Sardine Festival in Portimão. This event is a vibrant homage to one of the region's most beloved staples. The air fills with the aroma of sardines grilling over open flames, and the streets come alive with music and dance. It's an opportunity to join locals in a celebration that's as much about community as it is about food.

Beyond Seafood: While the Algarve is renowned for its seafood, the region's culinary repertoire extends far beyond the fruits of the sea. Traditional dishes like piri-piri chicken, spicy and succulent, or porco preto (black pork), rich and flavorful, showcase Algarve's diverse flavors. Local marketplaces are amazing gold mines of farm-fresh goods, cheeses, and cured meats, inviting you to taste the Algarve's agricultural heritage.

Culinary Experiences:

Cooking Classes**:** For those eager to delve deeper into the Algarve's culinary secrets, cooking classes are available throughout the region. Under the direction of regional chefs, learn how to cook traditional cuisine, and take a piece of the Algarve's culinary soul home with you.

Wine Tasting: The Algarve's winemaking tradition is as old as its hills, and visiting a local vineyard is essential for oenophiles. Sample robust reds and crisp whites, each telling the story of the sun-soaked terroir from which they sprung.

In the Algarve, every meal is an invitation to slow down and savor. From the simplest grilled sardine to the most elaborate seafood platter, dining here celebrates the region's rich maritime history and generous earth. So grab a seat, pour yourself a drink of the regional vinho verde, and toast to the culinary journey that awaits.

Cultural Experiences: Immerse yourself in the Algarve's rich heritage at the_Silves Medieval Fair, where history comes alive with re-enactments and artisan markets. Or, for a creative twist, join the workshops at the_Creative Loulé Festival and craft your piece of Algarve to take home.

Activities: Adventure awaits around every corner. Tee off at world-class golf courses or find serenity on the hiking trails of the Seven Hanging Valleys. For the thrill-seekers, the waves of Sagres beckon surfers from across the globe.

Contact Numbers:
- Faro Airport: +351 289 800 800
- AP Eva Senses: +351 289 001 000
- Stay Hotel Faro Centro: +351 289 898 080
- The Bold Octopus: +351 289 143 218

In the Algarve, every moment is a brushstroke on the canvas of your memories. So come, let the warm breeze guide you through a land where every sunset promises a new dawn of discovery.

1.2 Best Time to Visit Algarve

The Algarve, with its golden beaches and azure skies, is a canvas of experiences waiting to be painted by the eager traveler. As you plan your journey, consider the palette of seasons, each offering its hues and shades. As the Algarve emerges into the gentle warmth of spring, the region dons a cloak of vibrant colors and fragrances. The countryside is awash with the hues of wildflowers, and the air carries the promise of new beginnings.

Spring Splendor (April to May)

Weather: With temperatures averaging a comfortable 22°C, the climate is ideal for those looking to bask in the outdoors without the intensity of summer heat. The mild weather is perfect for long walks along the cliffs, where the Atlantic breeze is as refreshing as the panoramic views are inspiring.

Accommodation: The spring season offers excellent value, with 4-star hotels like the Hotel Algarve Casino in Portimão or the Vila Galé Marina in Vilamoura providing luxurious stays at around €100 per night. These hotels often feature spas, indoor pools, and gourmet restaurants, ensuring a restful and rejuvenating stay.

Outdoor Activities: This is a time when the Algarve's natural beauty is in full display, welcoming nature enthusiasts, bikers, and hikers to explore its varied landscapes. The Rota Vicentina trail network, for example, offers a variety of routes that take you through the heart of the region's flora and fauna.

Cultural Events: The Festival MED in Loulé is a highlight of the spring calendar, showcasing a fusion of musical genres from around the world. This celebration of multiculturalism is complemented by local crafts, gastronomy, and street performances, making it a feast for the senses.

Local Life: Spring also sees the return of local markets, where you can sample seasonal produce like sweet oranges and almonds. The markets are not just places to shop; they're social hubs where you can chat with friendly vendors and learn about the Algarve's agricultural traditions.

In the Algarve, spring is a season of joy and discovery. It's a time when the pace of life slows just enough for you to appreciate the details – the chirp of a bird, the scent of orange blossoms, and the sun's warmth on your skin. Whether wandering through ancient cobblestone streets or pausing to watch a sunset, spring in the Algarve is an experience that stays with you long after you've returned home. So come, embrace the season, and let the Algarve's springtime magic unfold around you. The Algarve's summer season is a symphony of sun, sea, and celebration. As the mercury rises, so does the vibrancy of this coastal haven, turning it into a bustling mosaic of tourists and locals alike, all seeking to soak up the best of what Portugal has to offer.

Summer Buzz (June to August)

Climate: The days are bathed in glorious sunshine, with temperatures averaging 28°C, creating the perfect conditions for sunbathing, swimming, and water sports. As the sun sets, the temperature gently dips to a pleasant 22°C, ensuring the evenings are as enjoyable as the days.

Beach Life: The Algarve's beaches, renowned for their golden sands and crystal-clear waters, become hubs of activity. From Praia da Rocha's family-friendly beaches to Praia da Marinha's quiet coves, there's a spot on the sand for everyone. Beachfront accommodations are in high demand, with prices starting at around €150 for a room with a view. It's wise to book early to secure your slice of paradise.

Culinary Delights: The Olhão Seafood Festival is a highlight of the summer calendar, where the ocean's bounty is celebrated with gusto. Indulge in grilled sardines, clams in white wine sauce, and the ever-popular cataplana. This gastronomic fiesta is accompanied by live music and dance, making it an unforgettable experience.

Marine Adventures: Take to the seas on a dolphin-watching tour, where you might glimpse these playful creatures leaping through the waves. The Algarve's coastline is a haven for marine life, and a boat trip provides a unique perspective on the region's natural beauty.

Festivals and Fun: Summer in the Algarve is a time of festivity, with events like the Lagos Jazz Festival and the Silves Beer Festival entertaining for all ages. Locals and tourists alike rejoice, filling the streets with music, laughing, and the clinking of glasses.

In the Algarve, summer is more than a season; it's a state of mind. It's where memories are made, friendships are forged, and the joys of life are savored to the fullest. Whether you're lounging on the beach, dancing at a festival, or marveling at marine life, the Algarve's summer buzz is an experience that will echo in your heart long after the tan fades. So, get your sunscreen, bring your appetite for adventure, and dive into the vibrant rhythm of Algarve's sunniest months.

Autumn in the Algarve is a season of mellow beauty, where the vibrant energy of summer gives way to a more peaceful tempo. It's a time when the region reveals its quieter side, inviting visitors to enjoy its many charms in a more intimate setting.

Autumn Calm (September to October)

Weather: The Algarve's climate remains generous, with daytime temperatures around 25°C. The sun still shines brightly, but its embrace is gentler, making it an ideal time for those who prefer the warmth without the peak summer heat.

Accommodation: As the high season wanes, the cost of staying in this picturesque region becomes even more appealing. You can find excellent accommodations for around €80 per night, offering great value for money. This is the perfect opportunity to stay in places like the Vila Vita Parc in Porches or the Pine Cliffs Resort in Albufeira, where luxury meets affordability.

Beach Escapes: The beaches, now less crowded, provide tranquil havens for long, reflective walks along the shore. The sea retains much of its summer warmth, inviting swimmers for a more secluded dip in the ocean.

Vineyard Visits: Autumn is harvest time, and the Algarve's vineyards are abuzz with activity. It's a fantastic time to visit local wineries like Quinta dos Vales or Adega do Cantor, where you can witness the grape-picking process and taste the region's finest wines.

Cultural Insights: The slower pace of autumn allows for deeper cultural immersion. Visit historical sites like the Castle of Silves without the summer crowds, or explore the Cork Route to learn about one of Portugal's most important industries.

Festivals: The season is rich with festivals, such as the Feira de Santa Iria in Faro, which celebrates local traditions with music, crafts, and food stalls offering regional delicacies.

Autumn in the Algarve is a time to savor the region's essence. It's an invitation to experience the local lifestyle, engage with the community, and appreciate the natural and cultural bounty that makes this corner of Portugal so special. Whether you're here to unwind or to explore, the Algarve in autumn offers a tapestry of experiences that weave together to form unforgettable memories.

Winter in the Algarve is a season wrapped in serenity and sprinkled with festive cheer. The region's authentic charm surfaces as the tourist tide recedes, offering a tranquil escape for those searching for calm and value.

Winter Whispers (November to March)

Tranquil Beaches: The Algarve's coastline, famed for its summer vibrancy, adopts a quieter demeanor. Stroll along the deserted shores of Praia de Odeceixe or Praia de Benagil, where your footsteps will probably be the only ones on the sand. The Atlantic remains invigorating, and a winter swim is a refreshing experience for the brave-hearted.

Affordable Stays: With the high season behind, accommodation prices become more inviting. Boutique guesthouses and charming B&Bs offer rates starting as low as €50 per night. Places like the Casa Modesta in Olhão or the Pensão Bicuar in Lagos provide cozy atmospheres that reflect the Algarve's warm hospitality.

Mild Climate: The Algarve's winter is gentle, with temperatures rarely dipping below 16°C. While the evenings may call for a sweater, the days are often bright and sunny, perfect for exploring the region's natural beauty without the summer heat.

Festive Atmosphere: December brings a festive glow to the towns and villages with twinkling lights and seasonal decorations. Traditional markets like the Vila Real de Santo António Christmas Market offer local crafts and treats, perfect for holiday shopping.

Cultural Exploration: Winter is an excellent time to delve into the Algarve's cultural offerings. Museums like the Museu Municipal de Faro and historical sites like the Castelo de Tavira are less crowded, allowing for a more personal experience.

Gastronomy: The cooler months are ideal for savoring the Algarve's hearty cuisine. Restaurants serve comforting dishes like feijoada (bean stew) and cozido à portuguesa (Portuguese stew), which pair wonderfully with the region's robust red wines.

In the Algarve, winter is a whisper of calm, an invitation to experience the region's soulful side. It's a time for reflection, for enjoying the simple pleasures of life, and for discovering the quieter, yet equally enchanting, rhythm of Portuguese coastal life. So come, wrap yourself in the Algarve's winter embrace, and find the peaceful retreat you've longed for.

Getting There: The Faro Airport is your gateway to this paradise, with frequent flights from major

European cities. Renting a car is advisable for the freedom to roam the scenic routes at your leisure.

Need Help? The Algarve Tourism Bureau (+351 289 800 400) is your compass for navigating this enchanting region, always ready to guide you towards your next adventure.

In the Algarve, every season sings its melody, and the best time to visit is the one that resonates with your travel rhythm.

1.3 Getting to Algarve

Embarking on a journey to the Algarve is like setting sail to a sun-drenched haven, where golden beaches and azure skies await your arrival. Whether you're craving the thrill of adventure or the solace of seaside serenity, the Algarve's southern embrace is just a voyage away. Faro Airport (FAO), also known as Algarve Airport, is conveniently located just four kilometers west of Faro. It's a traveler's delight, offering a range of facilities to ensure a smooth transition from air to land. You'll find information counters, medical services, ATMs, and baby care facilities to cater to your immediate needs. The airport provides free WiFi to keep you connected and tourist information to help you plan your stay. For a taste of local flavors or a quick bite, there are various restaurants and cafés within the airport.

In 2024, Faro Airport will enhance its connectivity by introducing a direct flight from New York to Faro, operated by United Airlines. Starting on May 24, this service is a game-changer for both leisure and business travelers alike, offering a convenient link between the bustling streets of New York and the tranquil beaches of the Algarve. The flights, scheduled four times a week, are set to depart from New York/Newark and arrive in Faro, bringing the Atlantic closer to you.

United Airlines Boeing 757-200 will carry passengers across the ocean with the choice of 16 flat-bed seats in United Polaris business class or 160 seats in economy, including 42 Economy Plus seats for those desiring extra comfort. With ticket prices starting at around €1,100 for Economy class and some Basic Economy tickets available for approximately €600, the new route offers options for various budgets.

Once you land, the Algarve awaits with open arms. This region is a tapestry of historic sites, scenic beaches, and cultural treasures. From the cobbled streets of Faro's Old Town to the dramatic cliffs of Sagres, every corner tells a story. Whether you're here to bask in the sun at Praia dos Pescadores or to explore the Sé Catedral De Faro, the Algarve is a destination that caters to every whim. Book your flight and let Faro Airport be the start of an unforgettable Portuguese adventure.

By Land: Journeying to the Algarve by land from Lisbon offers a picturesque prelude to your Portuguese escapade. The drive is a smooth 2.5-hour sojourn, spanning approximately 278 kilometers along the A2 motorway, which seamlessly transitions into the A22 as you approach the Algarve. The route is dotted with tolls, but with a ViaVerde pass, you can breeze through them without pause. This electronic toll collection system allows for a hassle-free drive, with charges directly debited from your linked account.

For those who revel in the allure of train travel, the Alfa Pendular and Intercidades services operated by Comboios de Portugal (CP) offer a comfortable journey from Lisbon to the Algarve. The Alfa Pendular is the swifter option, whisking you to your destination in about 3 hours, while the Intercidades take a leisurely 3.5 hours. Both services commence from Lisbon's Oriente or Entrecampos stations, with the rhythmic cadence of the train providing a soothing backdrop to the scenic vistas unfolding outside your window.

Whether you choose the independence of a car ride or the relaxed pace of a train, traveling to the Algarve from Lisbon is an experience that sets the tone for the leisure and discovery that await in this sun-kissed southern region of Portugal.

By Sea: Setting sail for the Algarve is to embark on a voyage through history and beauty. The region's marinas are not mere docking points but vibrant hubs of activity and gateways to the Algarve's rich maritime heritage. Lagos Marina was awarded the Euromarina Anchor Award, nestled in a bay that is one of the largest in Europe. It is steeped in a nautical tradition that dates back to the Age of Discoveries, reflecting the city's historical connection to the sea.

- Vilamoura Marina, the oldest in Portugal, is a bustling entertainment center, offering many dining and shopping options alongside its mooring facilities. It's a place where luxury yachts and local fishing boats create a picturesque mosaic against the backdrop of the Atlantic.

- Marina de Albufeira provides a colorful setting with its multi-hued buildings and various boat trips that invite you to explore the coastline and caves or to seek out dolphins in their natural habitat.

- For those seeking a more tranquil experience, Marina de Faro offers a charming and modest alternative, with a pleasant promenade that invites strolls.

Each marina in the Algarve has modern amenities to cater to the seafarer's needs. From fuel stations to repair services, showers, and laundry facilities, sailors can find all the conveniences required for a comfortable stay. Beyond the practicalities, the marinas serve as starting points for maritime adventures. You can take a sailing course at the Algarve Cruising Center or join a skippered sailing holiday to discover secluded beaches and the region's natural wonders.

As you glide into the Algarve's harbors, you're not just arriving at a destination; you're entering a story that unfolds with each wave and every breeze—a narrative the sea has written.

Local Tips:

- Faro Airport Contact: +351 289 800 800
- Train Information: CP - Comboios de Portugal, +351 707 210 220 (service available 24/7)
- Car Rental Tip: Check for the EASYToll system for a hassle-free toll experience.

As you plan your Algarve adventure, keep in mind that the trip is just as fascinating as the final destination. With each travel mode offering its unique narrative, how you get there might just become one of your fondest memories.

Chapter 2: Algarve at a Glance

2.1 Geography and Climate

Nestled at the southern tip of Portugal, the Algarve is a geographical wonder that beckons travelers with its stunning coastline and inviting climate. The Atlantic Ocean kisses golden beaches here, and the tranquil landscapes and craggy cliffs of the area are bathed in the gentle warmth of the sun.

Geography

The Algarve, Portugal's southernmost region, is a geographical marvel that captivates with its varied landscapes and natural beauty. The region's geography is a harmonious blend of contrasting terrains, each contributing to the Algarve's unique allure.

- **Monchique hills:** The Monchique hills, or Serra de Monchique, are a verdant oasis rising in the western part of the Algarve. These hills are renowned for their lush forests, an assortment of plants and animals, as well as the hot springs that have drawn tourists since the Roman era. The highest point, Fóia, stands at 902 meters, offering breathtaking panoramic views that stretch to the Atlantic coast.

- Eastern Algarve: Plains In stark contrast to the hilly west, the eastern Algarve is characterized by its vast, flat plains. This less developed and more serene area offers a glimpse into the traditional Algarvian lifestyle. The plains are dotted with charming towns like Tavira and Vila Real de Santo António, where time seems to move leisurely.

- **Algarve Coastline:** The Algarve's coastline is a spectacular symphony of nature's artistry, with over 200 kilometers of sandy shores, dramatic cliffs, and secluded coves. From the iconic Praia da Marinha with its natural rock arches to the surfer's paradise of Praia de Odeceixe, the coast offers a beach for every preference.

- Almond and Olive Groves Inland, the Algarve's countryside is adorned with almond and olive groves, a source of local produce and a part of the region's cultural heritage. The almond trees, particularly in bloom, create a stunning white landscape reminiscent of snow, a sight celebrated with traditional festivals. The olive groves, some with trees over a thousand years old, are a testament to the enduring agricultural practices of the region.

- The Algarve's geography is as diverse as it is picturesque, offering a tapestry of sights ranging from the serene hills of Monchique to the lively coastal towns, all connected by the tranquil beauty of its rural heartland.

Climate

The Algarve's climate is the quintessential Mediterranean idyll, offering a gentle winter reprieve and sun-soaked summer days. This region enjoys over 3000 hours of sunshine annually, outshining California's solar bounty.

- Winter in the Algarve is mild, with temperatures averaging around 12°C to 17°C. The cooler months may bring occasional showers, contributing to an average annual precipitation of 17.87 inches. These rains refresh the landscape, ensuring the Algarve's natural beauty remains lush and vibrant.

- As spring emerges, the mercury begins a steady ascent, with average temperatures in April hovering around 15°C. By May, the warmth is more pronounced, with averages of 17°C, setting the stage for the summer's heat.

- Summer in the Algarve is a time of vitality, with July being the hottest month, where temperatures can soar to an average high of 24°C. The sea becomes a welcoming retreat, with August sea temperatures averaging a delightful 21°C. It's a season made for basking on the beaches, with the sun reigning supreme for up to 12 hours a day.

- As autumn approaches, the heat subsides, but the region remains pleasantly warm. September's average temperature of 22°C gently transitions to the cooler yet agreeable 19°C of October.

The Algarve's climate is more than just numbers on a thermometer; it's a rhythm that dances to the tune of the seasons, inviting visitors to partake in its year-round charm. Whether seeking refuge from colder climes or chasing the perfect tan, the Algarve's weather is a reliable companion to your holiday narrative.
Seasonal Highlights

- **Summer (June to September):** Expect clear skies and temperatures soaring above 30°C. It's the season of sunbathing, water sports, and evening festivals.

- **Autumn (October to November):** The heat subsides, and the crowds disperse, leaving a tranquil atmosphere. It's the ideal time for hiking and enjoying the harvest.

- **Winter (December to February):** Cooler days and occasional rain make it perfect for exploring cultural sites and enjoying the local cuisine without the queues.

- **Spring (March to May):** Nature awakens with vibrant colors, and the weather is just right for outdoor adventures and discovering the Algarve's natural beauty.

Travel Tips

- **Getting There:** The Algarve is accessible by plane, with Faro Airport as the main gateway. Trains and buses connect the region to the rest of Portugal and Spain.

- **Stay Connected:** For inquiries and assistance, the Algarve Tourism Bureau (+351 289 800 400) is always ready to help plan your perfect getaway.

Embrace the Algarve's charm, where every visit promises discoveries and cherished memories under the Portuguese sun.

2.2 Culture and History

Step into the sun-drenched realm of the Algarve, where every corner tells a story, and history whispers from the ancient stones. In 2024, the Algarve's cultural tapestry is more vibrant than ever, inviting you to explore its rich past and lively present.

Silves Castle

Silves Castle, a majestic monument of the Algarve's Moorish past, stands proudly on a hill, offering a panoramic view of the town of Silves. Constructed from the region's distinctive red sandstone, the castle's walls and towers have withstood the test of time, echoing tales of conquest and culture. The castle dates back to the fourth or fifth century, with fortifications likely built by the Romans or Visigoths.

However, during the Moorish occupation, starting around 715, Silves Castle became prominent, serving as a formidable stronghold and part of the city walls. It was when Silves, known as Xelb, flourished as a center of trade and culture, becoming the capital of the Algarve region, then called Al-Gharb. Today, visitors can explore the castle daily from 9:00 to 17:30 for a modest entrance fee of €2.80. The castle's well-preserved walls, turrets, and gates testify to its 4.6-star rating, inviting guests to step back in time and immerse themselves in its storied past. For inquiries or to arrange a guided tour, contact the castle at +351 282 440 837.

The Silves Municipal Archaeological Museum is housed within the castle and is a veritable gold mine of relics that chronicles the history of the area from prehistoric times until the seventeenth century. The museum is particularly notable for its 12th-13th century Almohad cistern, a marvel of Islamic architecture and a rare example in Portugal, now a national monument. The museum's collections are organized chronologically, showcasing the region's prehistory, Roman, Muslim, and modern periods, with significant finds including Iron Age funerary stelae and a collection of Islamic ceramics.

Silves Castle is not just a historical site; it's an experience that connects visitors to the rich tapestry of the Algarve's past, offering insights into the lives of those who walked its ramparts and called it home. Whether you're a history enthusiast or simply seeking a picturesque escape, Silves Castle is a destination that promises to enchant and educate.

Lagos' Time Travel Experience

In the historic town of Lagos, the past is not merely observed—it's an immersive journey. The Half-Day

Lagos & Sagres Highlights Tour is a four-hour adventure that transports you to the Age of Discoveries, a pivotal era when intrepid explorers set sail to chart unknown territories.

This tour, rated at 4.3 stars, is priced at €48.88 promising a daily departure, ensuring flexibility for travelers. Convenient pickups are arranged, making the experience as seamless as possible. To secure your place on this voyage through time, contact +351 289 589 082. As you traverse the historical landscapes of Lagos and Sagres, you'll follow in the footsteps of the legendary navigator Gil Eanes. This fearless explorer, born in Lagos, was the first to sail beyond the daunting Cape Bojador, overcoming psychological barriers and opening the route for further exploration of Africa. His courage and determination symbolize the spirit that propelled Portugal to the forefront of maritime discovery.

During the journey, famous sites like the Fortaleza de Sagres are visited, a fortress that played a crucial role during the discoveries due to its strategic position in controlling the coast. You'll also witness the majestic Cabo São Vicente, the southwesternmost point of Europe, once believed to be the end of the known world. The powerful lighthouse stands as a beacon, much like it did for ancient mariners navigating treacherous waters.

This experience is more than a historical excursion; it's a tribute to the daring souls who shaped our understanding of the world. It's an invitation to touch history, to feel the salt air that filled the sails of caravels, and to gaze upon horizons that once held mysteries now revealed. Join the Half-Day Lagos & Sagres Highlights Tour and let the age-old discovery tales inspire your explorations.

Faro's Living History

Faro, the Algarve's capital, is where history breathes through the streets, and cultural experiences abound. The Algarve Life Sciences Center Museum is a beacon of learning, offering visitors a chance to delve into the region's rich biodiversity and historical narrative. Open daily, the museum charges a modest entry fee of €5.43, a small price for the wealth of knowledge housed within. With a 4.4-star rating, it's clear that this museum has captured the hearts of those who've wandered its educational halls. Contact the museum at +351 289 890 922 to arrange your visit.

The museum's exhibits celebrate the sea and its influence on the region, answering questions like "Why is the sea salty?" or "How are waves formed?". It's an interactive journey that takes you from the surface to the ocean's depths, revealing the secrets of life's origins and future on our planet.

For an evocative cultural experience, the Church of Mercy Fado Film and Live Performance offers a soul-stirring encounter with Portugal's traditional fado music. For just €10.32, you can immerse yourself in a 50-minute performance that showcases the melancholic melodies and expressive voices of fado artists. This performance is not just a show; it's a journey through the emotional landscape of Portuguese culture. To reserve your spot for this moving experience, call +351 289 824 490.

Fado, recognized by UNESCO as an Intangible Heritage of Humanity, is more than music; it's the story of Portugal told through song. The Church of Mercy, with its historic ambiance, offers the ideal environment for this private performance, where the haunting sounds of the Portuguese guitar accompany tales of love, loss, and longing.

In Faro, every corner turned is a step back in time, and every note heard is a piece of the soul laid bare. Whether you're exploring the depths of the sea at the museum or feeling the pulse of Portugal's heart through Fado, Faro invites you to live its history. These cultural beacons are easily accessible from any point in the Algarve, with public transport options and taxis readily available. Whether you're tracing the steps of ancient civilizations or soaking in contemporary culture, the Algarve in 2024 is a place where every moment is a memory in the making.

To Access Real Time Map Directions, Kindly Scan the QR Codes or Click on the Location Link to Get Accurate Map Directions.

2.3 Local Cuisine

As you meander through the cobbled streets of Faro, the scent of simmering seafood and the warm, inviting glow of restaurant windows beckon you to discover the Algarve's culinary soul. Here, the marriage of land and sea gives rise to a gastronomic palette as vibrant as the region's famed azulejos.

Restaurante Costa Algarvia

Discover the culinary heart of Faro at Restaurante Costa Algarvia, a cherished establishment that has been serving authentic Portuguese cuisine since 1971. This family-run restaurant is a tribute to the Algarve's gastronomic heritage, offering a menu brimming with traditional flavors and local ingredients.

Getting There: Restaurante Costa Algarvia is conveniently located at Rua Dom Francisco Gomes 13, Faro 8000-306, Portugal, just a short stroll from the picturesque Old Town Faro. Whether you're meandering through the city's historic streets or enjoying the waterfront at the marina, the restaurant is easily accessible for a delightful meal.

- Step into a world where each dish tells a story of the region's rich culinary past. The menu celebrates the Algarve's bountiful produce, from succulent seafood to hearty meat dishes. The atmosphere is cozy and welcoming, offering the choice of dining outside or in the cozy interior sitting area.

- Lunch at Restaurante Costa Algarvia is served daily from 12:00 to 15:00, while supper is served from 19:00 to 23:00, making it a perfect spot for both midday feasts and evening indulgences.

- With a capacity to accommodate up to 80 guests, the restaurant is ideal for intimate gatherings and larger groups. To ensure your spot, it's recommended to make a reservation by calling +351 289 878 174.

- Indulge in a range of dishes with prices that offer value for the quality and experience. The menu features items ranging from €21 to €41, ensuring something to satisfy every palate and budget.

- Restaurante Costa Algarvia holds a respectable 3.5-star rating, reflecting its commitment to quality and service. Guests often praise the restaurant for its flavorful dishes and the staff's attentive service.

Restaurante Costa Algarvia awaits your visit for a taste of the authentic and affordable Algarve. Whether you're a local or a traveler, this culinary gem promises a dining experience that will leave you with fond memories of Faro's gastronomic delights.

Faaron Steakhouse

Faaron Steakhouse stands as a beacon for grill enthusiasts in Faro, offering an array of exquisite cuts that cater to every palate. With a stellar 4.5-star rating, this steakhouse is not just a meal; it's a celebration of flavors.

Location & Accessibility: Nestled at Rua Ivens 9, Faro 8000-364, Portugal, Faaron Steakhouse is a mere 0.2 miles from Old Town Faro, making it an easy detour from your city exploration. Whether taking a leisurely walk through the historic streets or seeking a sumptuous reprieve after a day at the beach, the steakhouse is conveniently situated for all.

Cuisine & Offerings: Open from 10:00 to 23:00, except on Mondays, Faaron Steakhouse is a sanctuary for meat lovers and those with a penchant for varied culinary experiences. From the finest national and international cuts to a selection that satisfies snack lovers and vegan guests alike, their menu is a testament to inclusivity and quality.

Reservations: To ensure a seamless dining experience where the steaks rival the beauty of Algarve's sunsets, booking a table in advance is advisable. Make a reservation by calling +351 914 916 065.

Menu & Pricing: The menu at Faaron Steakhouse reflects its commitment to quality, with prices ranging from $11 to $38. This price point promises not just a meal but an experience that's worth every cent. For a dining experience where every bite is a journey through the rich tapestry of grilled delights, Faaron Steakhouse awaits your visit. Indulge in the grill sizzle and Faro's charm at this culinary haven.

Tertulia Algarvia

Tertulia Algarvia is not just a dining spot; it's a cultural hub where the flavors of the Algarve come to life. Located at Praça Dom Afonso III 13-15, Faro, this restaurant is a stone's throw away from the historical heartbeat of the city.

Getting There: If you're staying farther afield, you may take a brief cab trip to get to this gastronomic and cultural haven or stroll slowly through the quaint streets of Faro. The central location makes it easily accessible, and there's always a friendly local or a helpful map to guide you there.

Cuisine and Prices: Once you arrive, prepare to be greeted by a menu mosaic of the region's best. From nicely cooked pork cheeks to grilled octopus and tasty fruitcake, the offerings are a testament to the Algarve's bounty. With appetizers like "Merenda" priced at €4.60 and main courses that will entice your palate without going over budget, the pricing are as appealing as the food. Expect to spend around €16 - €65 for a filling and fulfilling meal.

Contact and Reservations: It's wise to book ahead to secure your spot in this popular locale, especially if you're planning to partake in their cooking classes or workshops. Call them at 289 821 044 to reserve your table or inquire about the day's activities.

With its 4-star rating, Tertulia Algarvia promises an experience rich in taste and steeped in the local narrative. So, whether you're there for the food, the culture, or both, you're in for a treat that's quintessentially Algarvian.

Each culinary star is a short stroll from Faro's central district, easily accessible by foot or a quick taxi ride. They're not just places to eat; they're chapters in the Algarve's gastronomic narrative, waiting for you to turn the page. So, as the Portuguese say, "Bom apetite!" – may your journey through the Algarve's flavors be as delightful as the adventures that await you under its sunny skies.

Chapter 3: Planning Your Trip

3.1 Visa and Entry Requirements

Embarking on a journey to the Algarve, the sun-kissed southern coastline of Portugal, is an adventure that begins long before you feel the warm sea breeze on your face. It starts with ensuring your paperwork is in order so your travels are as smooth as the sandy beaches awaiting your footprints.

Visa Essentials for Portugal: A Simplified Guide

Portugal, the land of age-old traditions and modern wonders, offers a seamless entry experience for many globetrotters. If you're from the European Union (EU), European Free Trade Association (EFTA), or European Economic Area (EEA), you're entitled to a hassle-free visit. Simply present a valid passport or ID card, and you're set to embark on a 90-day journey through Portugal's rich tapestry of cultural heritage and breathtaking landscapes. For those from the United States, Canada, Australia, New Zealand, or the United Kingdom, the warm embrace of Portuguese hospitality also extends to you. Experience 90 days of travel without a visa, taking in everything, from the calm beaches of the Algarve to the ancient alleys of Lisbon.

As you prepare for your Portuguese escapade, remember that this visa-free privilege allows you to traverse the entire Schengen Area. This means you can weave through the cobblestone alleys of Porto, marvel at the architectural splendor of Sintra, and indulge in the gastronomic delights of Coimbra, all on the same visa-free entry.

Should your travels extend beyond the allure of Portugal and into other Schengen territories, rest assured that your passport or ID card remains your key to unlocking the wonders of 26 additional European countries. For a journey that's as smooth as a glass of fine Porto wine, ensure your travel documents are up-to-date. Your passport must have been issued no more than ten years ago and be valid for at least three months after the day you want to leave the Schengen area.

If you're asked to provide additional documentation upon arrival, be prepared to show proof of sufficient funds, a return ticket, and accommodation details. These measures simply ensure that your stay is as planned and trouble-free as possible.

The Schengen Area is a remarkable free movement and travel zone encompassing 29 European countries.

Here's the list of countries where you can travel with a Schengen visa:
- Austria
- Belgium
- Bulgaria
- Czech Republic (Czechia)
- Croatia
- Denmark
- Estonia
- Finland
- France
- Germany
- Greece
- Hungary
- Iceland
- Italy
- Latvia
- Liechtenstein
- Lithuania
- Luxembourg
- Malta
- Netherlands
- Norway
- Poland
- Portugal
- Romania
- Slovakia
- Slovenia

- Spain
- Sweden
- Switzerland

These countries have abolished their internal borders, allowing for the unrestricted movement of people within the area. It's important to note that while Norway, Iceland, Switzerland,
and Liechtenstein are not members of the EU, they are part of the Schengen Area.

Additionally, Bulgaria and Romania recently joined the Schengen Area, further expanding the region of seamless travel. Enjoy your travels across these diverse and culturally rich countries! Embrace the spirit of adventure and let Portugal's charm unfold before you. Whether it's a short-term business trip or a leisurely holiday, the memories you create will be as enduring as the country's storied past.

But if your home country isn't on the visa-exempt list, don't fret. You'll need to apply for a Tourist Schengen Visa. This little document is your passport to Portugal and the entire Schengen buffet of 26 countries for any trip under 90 days within 180 days.

Application Process:

- **Photos**: Snap two passport photos with a grey background measuring 35×45 mm.
- **Passport**: Ensure it's no older than ten years and remains valid for at least three months beyond your planned farewell to the Schengen area.
- **Documentation**: Gather previous visas, a round-trip itinerary, proof of accommodation, and evidence of sufficient funds.
- **Cover Letter**: Compose a succinct account of your trip itinerary and the reason for your visit, being sure to include your contact information.

Costs and Timing: The visa fee is a small investment in your travel dreams. While the exact price can vary, it's typically around €80 for adults. During the busiest travel seasons, processing timeframes may take up to 15 days, so be sure you apply well in advance of your trip.

Where to Apply: You can start your visa application online, but you'll need to visit a consulate or visa application center in person to submit your documents. Find the nearest one by simply searching or contacting your country's Portuguese Embassy.

Pro Tips:

- **Contact Numbers**: Keep the number of the Portuguese Embassy handy, just in case you need assistance.
- **Travel Insurance**: It's not just a safety net; it's often a visa requirement, so don't skip it.
- **Stay Informed**: Rules can change, so always check the latest information before you pack your bags.

With your visa sorted, you're one step closer to sipping that glass of Vinho Verde on a terrace overlooking the Azure Atlantic. The Algarve's mosaic of cobbled streets, historic towns, and vibrant markets is ready to tell its tales. All you need is your passport to adventure. Boa viagem!

3.2 Health and Safety

As you sketch out the vibrant hues of your Algarve itinerary, let's sprinkle a dash of practicality with a pinch of care. The Algarve, a tapestry of azure skies and golden sands, is not just a feast for the eyes but a haven for the soul. Yet, even in this Portuguese paradise, it's wise to pack a little foresight alongside your sunscreen.

Exploring the Algarve: Your Comprehensive Transport Guide

Embarking on an Algarve adventure? You're in for a treat with the region's excellent infrastructure. Whether you're steering the wheel or letting someone else do the driving, here's what you need to know to navigate easily.

By Car: The Algarve's roads are a driver's dream—smooth and scenic. Renting a car gives you the liberty to explore at your own pace. You'll find two main thoroughfares: the A22 highway, a toll road that offers the quickest route between towns, and the N125, a national road that's free and perfect for leisurely drives with a view.

When renting a car, you'll have a variety of options to choose from. Most rental cars have an electronic device for the A22 tolls, making the process seamless.

Remember, driving in Portugal means staying within speed limits and always sober behind the wheel.

Public Transport: If you prefer to gaze out the window and soak in the sights, the Algarve's public transport system won't disappoint. Buses and trains are reliable and cover the entire region, ensuring you arrive on time.

Buses: Operated by three main companies—Próximo, Eva, and Frota Azul Algarve—buses are an economical way to travel. They're frequent, especially from Faro Airport to the city center, where you can catch bus 16 for a quick 20-minute ride. Remember to have some cash handy for tickets.

Trains: Comboios de Portugal (CP) runs services along the coast, connecting major towns like Lagos, Albufeira, and Faro. It's a scenic and comfortable option, especially for longer distances.

Taxis and Rideshares: For convenience, taxis and rideshare services like Uber and Bolt are available throughout the Algarve. They offer transparent pricing and can be a great choice for direct transfers or when public transport isn't an option.

Final Tips: No matter how you travel, the Algarve's transport options are designed to enhance your experience. With a little planning, you can ensure that getting from point A to B is just as enjoyable as the destination.

Sun-Kissed, Not Sunburned

The Algarve sun is generous, bestowing warm embraces that can turn harsh without proper care. Keep hydrated—water is your best friend, and sunscreen is your loyal ally. Apply it liberally, even when the clouds play peek-a-boo. And when the beach beckons, heed the flag warnings: red flags are not mere decorations but vital signals of the sea's mood.

Your Health Companion: Local Clinics and Pharmacies

Should you need medical attention, the Algarve's clinics and pharmacies are at your service. With English-speaking staff and no appointments for minor ailments, you can expect professional care without waiting. Here's a tip: keep the contact number of the nearest health center in your pocket—it's like carrying a little piece of mind with you.

Safety in Your Pocket: Emergency Numbers

112 is the number that unlocks assistance for any emergency. It's the key to immediate help, whether for

health cares or if you find yourself in an unexpected pickle. Save it on your phone; it's the number you'll hopefully never need but should always have.

Embrace the Algarve, Embrace Safety

In the Algarve, safety isn't just a sign on the wall; it's the invisible cloak that lets you confidently explore. From the cobbled streets of Faro to the serene cliffs of Sagres, let your spirit roam free, knowing that with a little caution, the Algarve is yours to cherish safely.

So there you have it, dear traveler. As you plan your journey, remember that the Algarve's embrace is warm, and with these health and safety tips, your trip will be as carefree as the coastal breeze. Bon voyage!

3.3 Budgeting for Your Trip

Embarking on a journey to the Algarve is like opening a book filled with colorful pages of adventure, relaxation, and cultural immersion. But before diving into this enchanting narrative, let's talk numbers and ensure your budget aligns with the experiences you seek.

Accommodation: Your home away from home in the Algarve can range from the AP Eva Senses, a 4-star hotel with a rooftop pool and marina views, starting at €100 per night, to the more economical Stay Hotel Faro Centro, where comfort meets affordability at €50 per night. Ratings and amenities are crucial, so choose a place that resonates with your comfort level and travel ethos.

Dining: Savor the local flavors without breaking the bank. A meal at Taberna Modesto offers the rustic charm of Portuguese cuisine, with dishes averaging €15. For a seaside dining experience, O Castelo provides a picturesque setting with meals for around €20. Remember, the taste of the Algarve is priceless, but it doesn't have to cost a fortune.

Transportation: Navigating the Algarve is a breeze, and there are options for every budget. Bus fares within cities like Faro start at €1.50, while a comprehensive 7-

day pass is around €22. If you prefer the independence of a car, while daily rates for rentals vary, one should budget around €30 for a modest automobile.

Activities: From exploring the mystical Benagil Caves on a boat tour for €35 to taking a stroll along the Seven Hanging Valleys for free, the Algarve offers a spectrum of activities. Allocate around €50 per day for experiences, and you'll have stories to tell for a lifetime.

Crafting a budget is the first step in your Algarve story. With a little planning, you can ensure that each chapter of your trip is as rich in experiences as it is in value. The Algarve awaits, ready to fill your days with golden memories that far outweigh their cost.

Chapter 4: Accommodation

4.1 Hotels and Resorts

Imagine waking up to the sound of waves gently lapping against the shore, the scent of salt in the air, and the warm Algarve sun peeking through your window. In the Algarve, your accommodation isn't just a place to sleep; it's part of the experience. Let's dive into some of the region's most inviting hotels and resorts where comfort meets the charm of southern Portugal.

AP Eva Senses: A Touch of Elegance in Faro

Immerse yourself in the elegance of AP Eva Senses, a hotel that epitomizes the blend of luxury and comfort. With a Tripadvisor rating of 8/10, this 4-star sanctuary is not just a place to stay; it's an experience designed to delight your senses.

Features & Amenities:

- **134 Rooms & Suites**: Each room is a haven of comfort, offering stunning views of the marina or the Ria Formosa Natural Park. Choose from

various rooms, including 13 suites tailored for families, groups, or solo travelers.
- **Dining**: Indulge in two restaurants with panoramic views and a rooftop bar (seasonal) where live music complements your favorite cocktails.
- **Health Club**: Guests over 16 can enjoy the modern Health Club, complete with a gym, group classes, sauna, and steam bath.
- **Day Spa**: Rejuvenate with relaxing treatments, deep massages, and personalized care at the Day Spa.
- **Outdoor Pool**: Open from May to October, the pool is a perfect spot to bask in the sun with a supporting bar offering a selection of cocktails and light meals.

Room Rates & Booking: Prices are competitive, ensuring that you get value for your experience. Contact the hotel directly at +351 289 001 000 for specific rates and availability.

Location & Accessibility:
- **Address**: Av. da República 1, Faro, Faro District, 8000-078.
- **Getting There**: The hotel is conveniently located just a **10-minute drive** from Faro Airport, making it easily accessible for travelers.

The Faro's Boarding Pier is also a short walk away, perfect for those exploring the Ria Formosa beaches.

Whether you're visiting for leisure or business, AP Eva Senses in Faro offers a touch of elegance and a promise of unforgettable memories. Book your stay and discover the allure of Faro's historic and commercial heart, all within steps from your luxurious retreat.

Hotel Faro & Beach Club: Where City Meets Sea

At the Hotel Faro & Beach Club, guests are treated to a seamless blend of city sophistication and coastal tranquility. This 4-star establishment, boasting an impressive rating of 8/10, is perfectly positioned for those wishing to soak up Faro's urban energy and tranquil beachside atmosphere.

Features & Offerings:

- **Accommodations**: The hotel features modern rooms and suites designed with comfort and style. Many rooms offer balconies with views that stretch over the marina and the Ria Formosa Natural Park.

- **Dining**: Savor the flavors of Portugal at the hotel's restaurant, which offers a panoramic vista of Faro's picturesque surroundings. The rooftop bar serves as an idyllic spot for evening cocktails accompanied by the soft serenade of live music.
- **Wellness**: A fully equipped fitness center and a serene outdoor pool cater to active guests and those seeking relaxation. The Day Spa invites you to indulge in a variety of pampering treatments.

Room Rates & Reservations:

- **Starting Price**: Competitive rates ensure guests receive exceptional stay value. For detailed pricing, please contact the hotel at +351 289 830 830.
- **Booking**: Reservations can be made through the hotel's website or by emailing the reservation desk at reservas@hotelfaro.pt.

Location & Accessibility:

- **Address**: Praça Dom Francisco Gomes 2, Faro, Faro District, 8000 -168.
- **Transport**: The hotel is conveniently located 7 km from Faro International Airport. The Faro train station and bus terminal are a mere 5-minute walk away, making it easily accessible for travelers.

Contact Information: For further details or to book your stay, contact the hotel at +351 289 830 830 or visit their. Whether you're in Faro for a leisurely escape or a business venture, Hotel Faro & Beach Club promises a stay that is as rejuvenating as it is inspiring. Embrace the harmony of city life and seaside leisure at this premier destination.

Finding Your Perfect Stay

Whether you're looking for luxury, a family-friendly environment, or a romantic getaway, the Algarve has many options to suit every taste and budget. From the bustling streets of Albufeira to the tranquil hideaways in Lagos, each hotel and resort is a unique chapter in your Portuguese story.

Remember, the Algarve's popularity means that the best spots fill up quickly, especially during summer. So, book early, pack your bags, and prepare to be swept off your feet by the region's hospitality. After all, in the Algarve, every guest is treated like royalty.

Check out the latest listings and traveler reviews for more detailed information on accommodations, including specific prices and availability. Don't hesitate to call your chosen hotel directly for any inquiries or special requests—they're always happy to ensure your stay is as magical as the Algarve itself.

4.2 Vacation Rentals

Imagine hearing the soft sound of the waves as you wake up, the scent of salt in the air, and the warmth of the Portuguese sun caressing your skin. In the Algarve, this isn't just a dream—it's what mornings look like when you choose the right vacation rental.

Palacete da Baixa by MY CHOICE

Discover the enchanting Palacete da Baixa by MY CHOICE, a charming accommodation that seamlessly blends the allure of Faro's historical essence with the comforts of modern living. With an impressive rating of 4.35, this delightful retreat is more than just a place to stay; it's an experience that promises comfort and style.

Starting from €75 per night, each of the 16 fully equipped apartments offers a sanctuary of relaxation and convenience. Imagine waking up in a space where every detail is curated for your well-being, from the satellite TV for your entertainment to the fully equipped kitchen where you can whip up a meal just how you like it.

But Palacete da Baixa is more than just its luxurious rooms. It's a gateway to the cultural heartbeat of Faro, located just a minute's walk from the city's vibrant riverfront and main shopping street. Step outside, and you're immediately immersed in the lively atmosphere of downtown Faro, with its rich history and picturesque settings.

For those eager to explore, the hotel's prime location near the pier is perfect for setting off on an adventure to the paradisiacal islands of the Ria Formosa. When the day is done, retreat to your haven, where comfort meets culture in a beautifully renovated building that echoes the charm of its surroundings.

Getting to Palacete da Baixa is a breeze, with the Faro Airport just 13 km away. The hotel provides a chargeable shuttle service to the airport, ensuring your journey to and from this slice of paradise is as smooth as possible. And for those arriving by other means, the bus terminal is within a 5-minute walk from the hotel, placing it within easy reach no matter how you travel.

To reserve your stay at this exquisite property, or if you have any inquiries, please contact +351 912 895 053 or email info@mychoice.pt. The dedicated staff are eager to assist you and ensure your unforgettable visit to Faro.

Embrace the unique blend of tradition and modernity at Palacete da Baixa by MY CHOICE and make your next trip to Faro a memory that will last a lifetime.

A Casa D'Amelie

Step into the heart of Faro and discover A Casa D'Amelie, where traditional charm meets contemporary comfort. With a stellar rating of 4.85, this boutique haven offers a tranquil escape with rates starting at just €65 per night.

Each air-conditioned unit at A Casa D'Amelie is a testament to thoughtful design and comfort. Enjoy the convenience of complimentary WiFi for visitors, ensuring you stay connected with the world, or choose to disconnect and bask in the serenity of your surroundings. The accommodations boast a fully equipped kitchen with a dining table, fridge, dishwasher, and microwave, alongside a coffee machine for your morning brew.

The rooms are more than just a place to sleep; they are a space where every detail has been considered for your utmost comfort. From the flat-screen TV with cable channels to the private bathroom stocked with complimentary toiletries and a hairdryer, each aspect of A Casa D'Amelie is designed to make you feel at home. Nestled just 90 meters from the city center, Casa D'Amelie's location is unbeatable. You're mere steps away from Faro's Cathedral, Lethes Theatre, and the picturesque Faro Marina. The property also features a charming terrace, perfect for soaking up the Algarve sun. Transportation is hassle-free, with Faro Airport only 13 km away. The home is conveniently close to the bus and rail terminals, both of which can be reached on foot, making it the perfect starting point for exploring the Algarve.

To book your stay or for any inquiries, contact A Casa D'Amelie at +351 965 100 259 or visit their website for more details. Embrace the allure of Faro and let A Casa D'Amelie be your home away from home.

ALGARVE TYPICAL DOWNTOWN HOUSE

Immerse yourself in the authentic charm of Faro with a stay at the ALGARVE TYPICAL DOWNTOWN HOUSE. This quaint abode rated 3.9, offers guests a unique glimpse into the Algarvian way of life, starting at an affordable €50 per night.

Nestled at Rua da Boavista 38, this downtown house is not just a place to rest; it's a cultural experience. The property boasts a good-sized house with two bedrooms, a comfortable lounge with TV, and a fully equipped kitchen. It's perfect for families or groups seeking a cozy, self-catering option in the city's heart. The location is second to none in the city center, offering easy access to Faro's historical sites, bustling markets, and vibrant nightlife. The house is a mere 10-minute stroll from Faro train and bus stations, making it incredibly convenient for travelers. Plus, with free parking on-site, guests arriving by car can enjoy peace of mind.

For those flying in, the Faro Airport is just 12 km away, and the property is within 400 meters of the city center, placing you at the doorstep of Faro's rich history and modern amenities. Everything is within reach, whether you're here to explore the Carmo Church & Bones Chapel, catch a show at the Lethes Theatre, or embark on a journey to the Island of Tavira.

To book your stay or for further inquiries, contact the ALGARVE TYPICAL DOWNTOWN HOUSE at +351 917 419 914. Prepare to be enchanted by the traditional architecture and the warm hospitality synonymous with the Algarve region. As you sift through the myriad options, remember that each vacation rental tells its story. Whether it's a traditional house's rustic allure or a modern apartment's sleek sophistication, your perfect Algarve retreat is waiting to be discovered.

4.3 Camping and Caravanning

In the Algarve, where the stars twinkle brighter, and the air smells sweeter, camping and caravanning are not just about a stay—it's about stories, the ones you'll tell for years to come. Let's wander through the groves and along the coast to find your perfect spot under the Algarve sky.

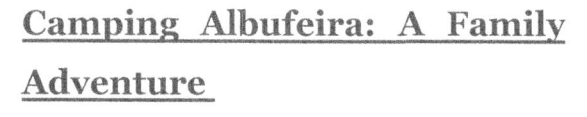

Camping Albufeira: A Family Adventure

Welcome to Camping Albufeira, where nature's embrace meets the comfort of home. This family-friendly site, with a 3.5-star rating, is a sanctuary for those looking to unwind amidst the beauty of the Algarve. Open daily from 09:00 to 21:00; it's a place where time slows down and life's simple pleasures take center stage.

- Accommodations at Camping Albufeira cater to all preferences, offering various options from pitching your tent on their lush grounds to parking your caravan in designated spots. For those who prefer a touch of solidity, caravans and bungalows are available, complete with two bedrooms, a bathroom with a hot shower, a living room, an equipped kitchenette, air

conditioning, and a TV. Linens and towels are provided, ensuring a comfortable stay.
- Prices are as inviting as the site, with options starting from a budget-friendly rate. For specific pricing details, contacting the site directly or checking their official price list is best.

- Facilities are abundant, ensuring your stay is both enjoyable and convenient. Guests can enjoy pools, a spa, beauty & massage services, self-service laundry, a supermarket, and various dining options, including restaurants and bars. For leisure, a padel court, a playground, and even bike and vehicle rental services are available.

- Entertainment is never far away, with live music and daily activities during the summer months ensuring that every day is fun and exciting.

- Getting to Camping Albufeira is easy, whether walking, biking, or driving. It's located just 1.5 km from the town and beach of Albufeira, with a bus stop at the entrance offering services every 30 minutes. The bus station is 2 km away, and the train station is 5 km away, with frequent buses to both stations.

- For more information or to book your stay, contact Camping Albufeira at +351 289 587 629. Whether seeking a peaceful retreat or a lively family holiday, Camping Albufeira offers the perfect backdrop for your Algarve adventure.

Camping Quarteira: Seaside Serenity

Nestled just 600 meters from the beach, Camping Quarteira offers a serene escape where the gentle murmur of the ocean is a constant companion. While it may not yet have a formal rating, its prime location on Avenida Francisco Sa Carneiro ensures a stay as peaceful as the sea. Camping Quarteira is a spacious park that caters to all camping enthusiasts, whether you're arriving with a tent, caravan, or seeking the comfort of a bungalow. The site features over 100 bungalows and mobile homes, all air-conditioned to ensure comfort during the warm Algarve days.

The accommodation options are diverse, with bungalows and mobile homes available in various sizes to suit different group sizes and preferences:

- **Azur Bungalow**: Suitable for four persons

- **Evasion Bungalow**: Perfect for two persons
- **Bungalow Club**: Accommodates five people
- **Morea Bungalow**: Also for five persons
- **Mobile Homes**: Including Neptune for larger groups and Venus for couples

Prices vary depending on the season, with different low, mid, and peak rates. For specific pricing, you are recommended to contact the site directly.

Camping Quarteira isn't just about a place to sleep; it's about the experience. The site boasts a swimming pool with slides, providing fun for all ages and an outdoor disco for evening entertainment. There's a restaurant, supermarket, and self-service facilities on-site for convenience. The campsite is open year-round, making it an ideal choice for summer and winter vacations. It has five health blocks and offers services like WiFi, a car wash, a playground, and even a first aid station.

Getting to Camping Quarteira is straightforward. For those driving, it's located at Estrada da Fonte Santa, Avenida Sá Carneiro – 8125-618 Quarteira – PORTUGAL. The campsite is accessible via GPS coordinates: N – 37° 04' 02" W – 008° 05' 14". For those using public transport, there's a bus stop nearby, and the site is well-connected to local amenities and attractions.

For inquiries or to make a reservation, contact Camping Quarteira at 289 302 826 or visit their website for more details. Whether you're looking for a family adventure or a quiet retreat, Camping Quarteira is your gateway to the perfect seaside holiday.

Lemon Tree Apartments - Faro: Urban Camping with a Twist

For those who love the city's heartbeat, the Lemon Tree Apartments in Faro offer an urban camping experience. With a 4.4-star rating, enjoy the comforts of home with the spirit of camping. Their contact? +351 918 604 040.

Embracing the Algarve's Natural Charm

The Algarve, Portugal's southernmost region, is a haven for campers and caravanners, offering a variety of sites that cater to every taste and preference. From the sun-kissed beaches to the tranquil countryside, here's what you can expect when you choose to stay at one of these delightful destinations:

Features & Amenities:

- **Family-Friendly Campsites:** Many sites offer a range of family facilities, including kids' clubs, playgrounds, and swimming pools.
- **Glamping Options:** For those seeking a more luxurious experience, glamping sites with yurts and treehouses are available.
- **Natural Beauty:** With over 125 miles of coastline, the Algarve boasts stunning beaches and a mild climate, perfect for outdoor activities.

Accommodations:

- **Variety of Pitches:** Whether you're bringing a tent, caravan, or motorhome, there's a spot for you. Some sites also offer bungalows and mobile homes for rent.
- **Prices:** Rates are budget-friendly, with options available for every financial plan. Prices vary depending on the season and the type of accommodation.

Transportation:

- **Accessibility:** Most sites are easily accessible by road, with clear signage leading the way.
- **Public Transport:** Local buses frequently run to popular camping sites, making it convenient for those without a vehicle.

Booking & Contact Information:

- **Advance Booking:** It's recommended to book your spot early, especially during peak season, to secure your preferred site.
- **Contact Numbers:** Each site has a dedicated contact number for inquiries and reservations. For example, Camping Albufeira can be reached at 289 587 629, and Camping Quarteira at 289 302 826.

Ratings:

- **Guest Reviews:** Visitors have rated many sites, providing insight into the quality of the facilities and services.

When planning your trip, consider the type of experience you're looking for. Whether it's a family holiday filled with activities or a peaceful retreat into nature, the Algarve's camping and caravanning sites are equipped to provide an unforgettable experience. Remember to check the specific features of each site, as they can vary widely, from seaside views to countryside serenity. Embrace the Algarve's natural charm and book your patch of paradise early to avoid missing out on these coveted spots. Happy camping!

And there you are, ready to embark on a journey where the nights are a canvas of stars and the days are filled with exploration. In the Algarve, every camper and caravanner finds a home.

Chapter 5: Transportation

5.1 Getting Around Algarve

Navigating the Algarve is a breeze, whether zipping through the coastal roads or hopping on a bus to the next sun-kissed village. In 2024, the region's transport network is your golden ticket to an effortless adventure.

Direct Algarve Shuttle

Welcome to the Algarve, where your journey begins with the convenience and comfort of the Direct Algarve Shuttle. This esteemed shuttle service operates daily from 08:00 to 19:00, ensuring a seamless and stress-free transition from air to road travel. Upon your arrival at Faro Airport, the Direct Algarve Shuttle awaits to deliver you to the doorstep of your holiday destination. With a 3-star rating, this service prides itself on its commitment to transparency, safety, and comfort. The fleet of well-maintained vehicles is equipped to cater to all your transportation needs, ensuring a pleasant ride through the scenic vistas of the Algarve.

Booking your shuttle is quite easy; simply call +351 919 339 777 to secure your seat. The friendly staff are ready to assist you, providing clear instructions and support throughout the booking process. Whether you're traveling solo or with family, the Direct Algarve Shuttle accommodates all group sizes, and special arrangements, such as child car seats, are available upon request to ensure the safety of your little ones.

As you embark on your Algarve adventure, rest assured that the Direct Algarve Shuttle is dedicated to starting your holiday on the right note. With competitive rates and a focus on customer satisfaction, they are a preferred choice for travelers seeking a reliable and enjoyable transportation experience from Faro Airport to the Algarve's vibrant towns and serene beaches.

Remember, your comfort and convenience are just a phone call away with the Direct Algarve Shuttle—where every journey is more than just a ride; it's the beginning of your unforgettable Algarve experience.

EVA - TRANSPORTES, SA

Embark on a journey through the Algarve's picturesque landscapes and charming towns with EVA - TRANSPORTES, SA. This bus service is the lifeline for locals and travelers, offering a reliable and affordable way to explore the region's rich tapestry.

Operating Hours:

- **Monday to Friday**: 08:30 to 17:30

- **Weekends**: Schedules vary, providing flexibility for weekend excursions.

Despite its modest 2-star rating, EVA's buses are an integral part of daily life in the Algarve, weaving through the region's towns and villages with a steadfast rhythm. The buses serve as a window to the Algarve's soul, connecting not just places but also people and experiences.

Contact Information:

- **Phone**: 289 899 700
- **Address**: Avenida da República 5, Faro, Continental Portugal, 8000

Travelers can expect a straightforward service that, while lacking in luxury, delivers on consistency and coverage. The buses are equipped to handle the diverse needs of its passengers.

EVA's buses provide a unique vantage point for those looking to delve deeper into the Algarve's hidden gems. From the comfort of your seat, watch the landscape unfold, revealing everything from bustling market towns to serene coastal views.

Booking and Navigation:

- **Advance Booking**: This is not typically required but is recommended during peak travel seasons.
- **Navigation**: Familiarize yourself with the routes and stops to maximize your travel experience.

While EVA - TRANSPORTES SA, may not boast the highest rating, it stands as a testament to the Algarve's welcoming spirit and commitment to accessibility. It's not just a mode of transport; it's a passage to discovery, inviting you to uncover the Algarve's wonders one stop at a time.

Nmr - Algarve Shuttles

Nmr - Algarve Shuttles stands out as a premier transportation service in the Algarve region, boasting a commendable 4.4-star rating. This company is renowned for its commitment to providing a bespoke travel experience, ensuring each journey is tailored to its client's needs and preferences.

With a modern and well-maintained vehicle fleet, Nmr - Algarve Shuttles promises comfort and reliability. In case you're planning to explore the bustling streets of Faro, the historic charm of Silves, or the serene beauty of Alcoutim, their service is designed to take you to some of the Algarve's most treasured locations. The drivers at Nmr - Algarve Shuttles are skilled in navigation and known for their warm and approachable demeanor. They serve as informal ambassadors to the region, ready to share insights and recommendations to enhance your travel experience.

To book a ride and discover the Algarve's hidden gems, contact Nmr - Algarve Shuttles at 962 483 750. Their responsive team will assist you in planning your itinerary, ensuring you have a memorable journey through this picturesque corner of Portugal. As you traverse the Algarve with Nmr-Algarve Shuttles, you'll have the opportunity to uncover hidden beaches, quaint villages, and local markets off the beaten path. The Algarve is not just a destination; it's an experience waiting to be savored, and Nmr - Algarve Shuttles is your key to unlocking its full potential.

Public Buses and Trains

The Algarve's public transportation system is a seamless blend of convenience and affordability, designed to enhance your exploration of this enchanting region. With bus fares starting as low as €1.50 and not exceeding €5.00, the cost-effectiveness of this travel option is unmatched. Three main companies in the Algarve operate Buses: Próximo, Eva, and Frota Azul Algarve. They connect all the major towns and cities, ensuring a bus route to get you there, whether you're heading to a bustling market or a tranquil beach. The buses are known for their punctuality, mirroring the rhythmic flow of the Algarve itself. They are a reliable choice for travelers who value the journey as much as the destination. The train network offers a scenic passage through the Algarve's landscapes for those who prefer the rails. A single railway line runs from Lagos in the west to Vila Real de Santo António in the east, with stops at key locations along the coast. The trains provide a slower but more picturesque travel alternative, allowing you to witness the region's beauty unfold from your window seat.

The regional trains are the most cost-effective and make stops at every station, offering a comprehensive tour of the Algarve's coastal stretch. Meanwhile, the Intercidades (IC) trains provide faster travel between the Algarve and Lisbon, with convenient connections to regional trains covering the region's east and west. If you decide to choose the bus or train, each mode of transport in the Algarve is an invitation to immerse yourself in the local culture and scenery. As you hop from one stop to the next, the soul of the Algarve reveals itself, one journey at a time. Grab a ticket, find a seat, and let the Algarve's public transportation take you on an adventure through the heart of Portugal's southernmost region.

5.2 Public Transportation

Navigating the Algarve's public transportation is like discovering a hidden path in a lush garden; it's part of the adventure. The region's network of buses and trains is your key to unlocking the treasures scattered along this picturesque coastline.

Buses - The Heartbeat of Algarve Transit: The bus system in the Algarve is your reliable companion, ready to whisk you away from the early morning light until the stars take the stage. With routes connecting the dots between towns and cities, you're never far from your next discovery. Prices are as friendly as the locals, ranging from €1.50 to €5.00, depending on your journey's length. And for those who find themselves enamored with the Algarve's charm, discounted passes will make your travels even sweeter.

Trains - Scenic Journeys Along the Coast: The train is a movable perspective as well as a means of transportation. Gliding along the coast, you'll be treated to a visual feast of the Atlantic's azure waters and the rugged cliffs. The trains are your cool oasis, air-conditioned to comfort you as the Algarve sun pours its warmth. The coastal train network is your ticket to a scenic route, with prices that won't break the bank.

Ferries - Float to Your Next Adventure: Don't forget the ferries, the unsung heroes that connect you to the Algarve's islands. They're the bridges over the ocean, taking you to sandy sanctuaries away from the mainland bustle.

Pro Tips:

- **Timetables**: Check online or at the stations for the latest schedules to plan your day seamlessly.
- **Travel Cards**: If you're staying a while, look into travel cards for discounts that'll have you hop on and off easily.
- **Contact Numbers**: Save the number of the local transport line for any inquiries or assistance during your travels.

With public transportation this accessible, every corner of the Algarve is within reach. Whether heading to a hidden beach cove or a hilltop village, the journey is as delightful as the destination.

5.3 Car Rentals

The Algarve's roads are your gateway to discovery, and what better way to traverse this scenic landscape than in the comfort of your rental car? With the freedom of four wheels, every hidden beach, cliffside vista, and quaint village becomes a part of your Portuguese tale.

Drive4Miles Rent a Car: Your Journey Begins Here

Embark on a seamless journey with Drive4Miles Rent a Car, where your satisfaction is the cornerstone of their service. With an impeccable 5-star rating, this esteemed establishment in Faro is renowned for its commitment to excellence and customer care.

Nestled in the heart of Faro, you can find Drive4Miles at Av. da República 168, Loja 5. This prime location is easily accessible and the perfect starting point for your Algarve adventure. Should you need to discuss your rental options or require assistance, a friendly voice is just a phone call away at +351 913 303 351. Drive4Miles boasts a diverse fleet, guaranteeing that your requirements are satisfied with the highest level of care, whether you're seeking a compact car for city driving or a spacious vehicle for family excursions. From economical Group B models starting at 31.43€ to the more robust Group G options at 74.29€, there's a car for every budget and purpose.

At Drive4Miles, the journey is just as important as the destination. Their customer-oriented service includes free airport pickup and a transparent pricing policy with no hidden taxes. You're not just renting a car; you're being taken care of by a team that values your experience above all. Each vehicle in the Drive4Miles fleet comes equipped with air conditioning, ensuring your comfort in the warm Algarve climate. With a range of manual and automatic options, you can choose the driving style that best suits your preferences.

Drive4Miles Rent a Car invites you to begin your exploration of the stunning Algarve region with confidence and ease. Their dedication to excellence and client satisfaction, you're not just renting a car but embarking on an unforgettable journey. Visit their website or stop by their Faro location to start your adventure.

Nice Rent: Smooth Sailing on Your Algarve Journey

At Nice Rent, the promise of a smooth ride is not just a slogan—it's a commitment. With a 5-star service rating, they stand as a beacon of reliability in the car rental industry. Their fleet, a testament to their dedication, is as dependable as the service they offer. Conveniently located near Faro Airport at Rua Poeta Antonio Aleixo Nº 13, Montenegro, Faro, Nice Rent positions itself as the ideal starting point for your travels in the Algarve. The proximity to the airport means you can transition from flight to car with minimal delay.

Their doors are open every day of the week, from 08:30 to 18:00, with a scheduled break from 12:30 to 14:00. This schedule caters to a wide range of travel plans, ensuring that Nice Rent is available when needed. Whether you are looking for an elegant car for city zipping or a spacious SUV for scenic drives, Nice Rent's diverse fleet has you covered. Each vehicle promises comfort and safety, ensuring peace of mind as you navigate the beautiful Algarve.

At Nice Rent, every customer is a VIP. Reach out at 912 562 700 and experience their renowned customer service that makes every interaction a pleasure. Choose Nice Rent for your car rental needs and confidently embark on your Algarve adventure. They're more than just a rental service; they're your partner in exploration. Visit them and see why their name says it all.

Enjoy2Drive: Customized Car Rental Experience in Faro

Embark on a journey filled with character and charm with Enjoy2Drive. Since its establishment in 2019, this Faro-based car rental service has swiftly risen to prominence, boasting a 5-star rating for its exceptional service and customer satisfaction. Located at Rua Bernardino Bonixe, 1 1ºesq., Faro, Enjoy2Drive offers convenient access for travelers eager to explore the Algarve's picturesque landscapes and vibrant cities.

Dial 912 133 527 and connect with Enjoy2Drive's dedicated team, they are prepared to help you choose the ideal car that fits your needs and travel preferences. In case you're organizing a family holiday or a solitary excursion, Enjoy2Drive's diverse fleet includes everything from the agile Citroën C1 to the family-friendly Dacia Jogger 7 Seat. Each car is meticulously maintained to ensure your safety and comfort on the road.

Enjoy2Drive stands out for its transparent pricing with no hidden costs, ensuring a stress-free rental experience. Additionally, they offer premium services like 24/7 assistance, full damage coverage, and the convenience of car delivery to your preferred location.

With glowing reviews praising their VIP treatment and responsive support, Enjoy2Drive is not just a car rental company; it's a gateway to an unforgettable Algarve adventure. Choose Enjoy2Drive for a personalized service that turns every trip into a memorable journey.

Freedom on a Budget: Algarve's Car Rentals for Every Wallet

The Algarve, known for its stunning coastline and picturesque towns, offers a variety of car rental options to suit every traveler's budget. Whether you want to save or indulge, you'll discover the ideal car to enhance your travels. For the budget-conscious, economy cars are available for as little as $8 daily. These vehicles are a cost-effective way to navigate the region's charming streets and are perfect for solo travelers or couples.

If you want to treat yourself, consider renting a convertible for about $17 daily. There's nothing quite like cruising along the Algarve's scenic routes with the top down, feeling the warm breeze as you soak in the

Mediterranean sun. Remember that rental prices can increase significantly during the Algarve's peak tourist season. To avoid the rush and secure the best rates, booking your car rental well in advance is wise.

Beyond economy and convertible cars, the Algarve offers a range of other rental options, including family-friendly SUVs, sporty models, and luxury vehicles. Rental companies provide various deals, ensuring you can find a car that fits your needs and wallet.
The roads in the Algarve are well-maintained, making it easy for drivers to explore the region safely. Car rental agencies often offer additional services like GPS navigation to help you find your way around without hassle.

Renting a car in the Algarve allows you to discover hidden beaches, historic sites, and local markets at your own pace. With options for every budget, you can enjoy the beauty of the Algarve without worrying about the cost. Remember to book early, especially during the busy season, and prepare to embark on an unforgettable road trip through one of Portugal's most beloved regions.

In the Algarve, every road is a story, and every rental car is a potential chapter in your travelogue. So, pick your ride, plot your course, and let the open roads of Portugal lead you to memories that will last a lifetime

Chapter 6: Itinerary

6.1 Day 1: Arrival and Exploring Faro

Welcome to Faro! Your Algarve adventure begins in Faro, the region's captivating capital. As you step off the plane and breathe in the coastal air, you're ready to dive into the heart of Portuguese charm.

Morning: Arrival and Settling In

- **Faro Airport**: Your gateway to the Algarve, just a short taxi ride (approximately €10-€15) or bus trip (around €2.50) from the city center.
- **Accommodation**: Check into your chosen hotel, like the centrally located AP Eva Senses (4-star, from €120 per night, with a rooftop pool and marina views) or the budget-friendly Best Western Hotel Dom Bernardo (3-star, from €80 per night, offering a cozy stay).

Afternoon: Cultural Immersion

- **Old Town**: Wander through cobbled streets and discover the neoclassical Arco da Vila. Entry is free, and it's open all day.

- **Faro Cathedral**: Marvel at this architectural gem from 1251. Admission is around €3, open from 10:00 AM to 6:00 PM.
- **Museu Municipal**: Explore Faro's history with a visit to this museum housed in a 16th-century convent. Entry is €2, open from 10:00 AM to 7:00 PM.

Evening: Gastronomic Delights

- **Dining**: Treat yourself to a culinary journey at EPICUR - Wine Boutique & Food (Fusion cuisine, around €20-€30 per person, open until 2:00 AM), or enjoy the vibrant atmosphere at Columbus Culinary Bar (Gastronomic delights with a local twist, meals from €15-€25, open until 4:00 AM).

Night: Unwind and Reflect

- **Stroll by the Marina**: As the sun sets, take a leisurely walk along the marina, reflecting on the day's experiences.
- **Rooftop Drinks**: Cap off your night with a cocktail at your hotel's rooftop bar overlooking the twinkling lights of Faro.

Contact Numbers:

- Faro Airport: +351 289 800 800

- Best Western Hotel Dom Bernardo: +351 289 889 800
- EPICUR - Wine Boutique & Food: +351 935 194 099
- Columbus Culinary Bar: +351 969 286 222

Faro is more than just a stopover; it's a treasure trove of culture and cuisine waiting to be discovered. Rest well, for tomorrow, the Algarve reveals more of its secrets.

6.2 Day 2: Lagos and Ponta da Piedade

Embrace Lagos's coastal charm and Ponta da Piedade's natural splendor on your second day. This itinerary is crafted to immerse you in the beauty and culture of one of the Algarve's most picturesque areas.

Morning: Stroll Through Lagos' Old Town

Start your day with a stroll through the cobbled lanes of Lagos' Old Town. The history here is palpable, with each building telling tales of seafarers and explorers. The town wakes up early, with shops opening by 9:00 AM. Enjoy a coffee at a local café and watch the town come to life.

Mid-Morning: Visit the Lagos Market By 10:00 AM and go to the bustling Lagos Market. A wide selection of locally made goods and fresh vegetables may be found here. It's a vibrant spot where the community's heart beats strongly, and you can pick up some snacks later in the day.

Lunch: Head to O Camilo, a restaurant perched above the stunning Camilo Beach. With a 4.5-star rating, it provides a sensory feast. Operational hours: 12:00 PM – 10:00 PM you can indulge in seafood delights with dishes averaging around €15-€25. Call +351 282 763 845 to book a table with a view.

Afternoon: Ponta da Piedade Boat Tour

After lunch, it's time to explore the breathtaking cliffs and caves of Ponta da Piedade. Join a boat tour leaving from Lagos Marina at 2:00 PM. The tours, rated 4.7 stars, last about 2 hours and cost approximately €20 per person. For bookings, contact +351 282 770 550.

Late Afternoon: Hike to the Lighthouse

Post boat tour and hike up to the Ponta da Piedade Lighthouse. The walk takes about 30 minutes from the marina and offers stunning views. The lighthouse doesn't charge an entry fee and is open until sunset.

Dinner: Sunset and Savory Delights

Conclude your day at Restaurante dos Artistas, located in the heart of Lagos. With a 4.6-star rating, it's a culinary canvas of Portuguese flavors. They're open from 6:00 PM to 12:00 AM, and dinner averages €30-€40 per person. Secure a spot for sunset dining at +351 282 760 659.

Getting There: Lagos is well-connected by public transport, but to fully enjoy this itinerary, consider renting a car or using local taxis. Car rentals start from around €25 per day, and taxi fares within Lagos are reasonable, with most rides under €10.

This day promises cultural exploration and natural wonder against the Algarve's stunning coastline. It's a day to remember, filled with flavors, sights, and the soothing sounds of the sea.

6.3 Day 3: Silves and Monchique

Morning in Silves:

1. Start your day with a visit to Silves Castle, a majestic remnant of the Moorish rule, with a 4.5-star rating.
2. Open from 9 AM to 5 PM, the castle invites you to wander through its red sandstone walls and offers panoramic town views for an entry fee of €2.50.
3. For inquiries, call +351 282 440 837.

Next, stroll down to the Silves Cathedral, just a few minutes away, open from 9 AM to 6 PM. Its Gothic architecture and modest entry fee of €1.50 make it a serene spot to reflect on the town's rich history.

Lunch in Silves: For lunch, indulge in local flavors at Café daRosa. Their seafood dishes are a delight, and with a 4.7-star rating, your taste buds are in for a treat. They're open from 12 PM to 3 PM, and you can reserve a table at +351 282 442 585.

Afternoon in Monchique: In the afternoon, drive up to Monchique, approximately 30 minutes from Silves. Visit the Caldas de Monchique, a thermal spa with a history dating back to Roman times. The spa is open from 10 AM to 6 PM, you can rejuvenate with treatments starting at €35. Contact them at +351 282 910 910.

Evening at Fóia: Conclude your day at Fóia, the highest peak in the Algarve. The drive-up offers breathtaking views, and the summit is perfect for sunset. There's no entry fee, and the mountain is accessible until dusk. For the adventurous, guided hikes are available with Algarve Trails; contact +351 289 123 456 for booking.

As the stars begin to twinkle, reflect on the day's journey — the historical whispers of Silves and the natural allure of Monchique. It's not just a day spent; it's an experience etched in memory.

6.4 Day 4: Tavira and Ria Formosa

Morning: A Gateway to Nature - Tavira

Start your day in the tranquil town of Tavira, a gem that retains its traditional charm. Wander through the cobbled streets and take in the sights of the historic Roman bridge and the medieval castle ruins. For breakfast, stop by Tavira Lounge (Contact: +351 281 325 460) and enjoy a local pastry with a view of the Gilão River.

Midday: Ria Formosa Natural Park

As the sun climbs, go to the Ria Formosa Natural Park. This coastal lagoon is a haven for wildlife and a paradise for birdwatchers. Visit the park's visitor center (Open: 10:00 - 17:00, Contact: +351 289 700 210) to learn about the area's ecology. Don't miss the restored Tide Mill, now a fascinating museum.

Afternoon: Island Hopping

Board a ferry to explore the barrier islands of Ria Formosa. Each island offers its unique slice of heaven, from the deserted beaches of Ilha Deserta to the vibrant community of Ilha da Culatra. Ferries run regularly from Tavira; a round trip will cost around €20 per person.

Evening: Culinary Delights

Conclude your day in Tavira with a seafood feast at Marisqueira Fialho (Open: 19:00 - 23:00, Rating: 4.5/5, Contact: +351 281 324 567). Savor the day's fresh fish that has been perfectly grilled and seasoned with Algarven tastes.

Traveler's Note:

- **Prices:** Expect to spend around €50-€70 per person for a full day's activities, including meals and transportation.
- **Getting There:** Tavira is well-connected by train and bus services from major cities in the Algarve. The town is just a 30-minute drive from Faro.

Immerse yourself in the natural and cultural splendors of Tavira and Ria Formosa, where each moment is a brushstroke on the canvas of your Algarve memories.

6.5 Day 5: Sagres and Cape St. Vincent

Awaken your spirit of adventure on Day 5 as you set out to explore the rugged beauty of Sagres and the mythical edge of Europe, Cape St. Vincent. This corner of the Algarve is steeped in legends and breathtaking views, offering a day where every moment is a postcard waiting to be captured.

Morning: Fortress of Sagres

Begin your day at the Fortress of Sagres, a monument that is a sentinel to Portugal's Age of Discoveries. Operating hours: 10:00 – 18:00 with an entry fee of €3.50, this fortress offers panoramic views that stretch out into infinity. Rated 4.7 stars, it's a place where history's echoes are almost audible. Call +351 282 620 140 to inquire about guided tours that can enrich your visit.

Lunch: A Marisqueira

After your historical exploration, indulge in the freshest catch at A Marisqueira, a seafood haven with a 4.5-star rating. Nestled in the heart of Sagres, they serve up a symphony of flavors from 12:00 to 15:00. To have a dinner that really captures the essence of the sea, budget between €20 and €30 per person. Reserve your table at +351 282 624 788 and savor the essence of the ocean.

Afternoon: Cape St. Vincent Lighthouse

As the afternoon sun casts golden hues over the cliffs, make your way to the Cape St. Vincent Lighthouse. Open from 10:00 to 18:00 on Monday through Sunday, with a fee of €1.50, it's a beacon that has guided sailors for centuries. With a 4.8-star rating, the lighthouse is not just a landmark; it's a symbol of the Algarve's enduring spirit. Contact +351 282 624 875 for more information on the lighthouse's fascinating history.

Sunset: The End of the World

Conclude your day where the land ends and the vast Atlantic begins. The sunset at Cape St. Vincent is an experience that transcends words. Rated as one of the most stunning sunsets with a 5-star rating, it's a moment where time stands still, and the sky paints masterpieces. No contact number is needed here—just bring your camera and your sense of wonder.

Getting There: Sagres and Cape St. Vincent are accessible by car, with ample parking. If you prefer public transport, there are three daily buses from Lagos to Sagres, with the last stop at Cape St. Vincent. For a hassle-free day, consider booking the Sagres & Cape St. Vincent Half-Day Tour from Lagos, which includes hotel pickup and drop-off.

This day in the Algarve is more than an itinerary; it's a journey through time, nature, and the soul-stirring landscapes that define this southwestern tip of Europe. Let the Algarve's rugged charm lead you to discoveries both within and beyond.

6.6 Day 6: Albufeira and Surroundings

Wake up to the promise of adventure in Albufeira, a town where the sun paints the sky in hues of hope and the ocean whispers tales of old. Today, you'll weave through the vibrant tapestry of Albufeira's streets and its surroundings, where every corner offers a story, and every moment is a memory in the making.

Morning - Old Town Charms:

1. Start your day in the heart of Albufeira's Old Town.
2. Stroll through the cobbled lanes as the sun stretches its golden fingers over the whitewashed buildings.
3. Pop into a local café, where the scent of freshly baked pastéis de nata beckons.

For just €1-2, these little custard tarts will sweeten your morning.

Midday - Marina Marvels: Make your way to the colorful marina by midday. Here, you can embark on a dolphin-watching cruise (€30-40 per person) that promises a ballet of marine life against the backdrop of the vast Atlantic. The cruises usually set sail around 10 AM and 3 PM, but it's best to book in advance and check for the exact times.

Afternoon - Beach Bliss: In the afternoon, surrender to the allure of Praia dos Pescadores, where the sands are as warm as the local hospitality. Beach umbrellas dot the landscape, available for rent at around €10-15 for the day. The beach is a short walk from the Old Town, inviting you to dip your toes into the ocean's embrace.

Evening - The Strip's Vibrance: As evening falls, The Strip awakens. This is Albufeira's famous party street, where themed bars and nightclubs pulse with life. Dinner at a local restaurant will cost around €15-25 per person, promising savory seafood and a symphony of lively conversations.

Night - Stargazing Serenity: End your day under the stars at one of Albufeira's rooftop bars. With a cocktail in hand (around €5-8), let the night sky tell its ancient stories as you reflect on a day well spent.

Pro Tips:

- **Contact Numbers**: Keep the tourist information center number (+351 289 580 800) on speed dial for inquiries.
- **Transportation**: Local taxis are readily available, and a ride within the town typically costs €5-10.

- **Accommodation**: Book your stay in advance, especially during summer, to secure the best spots.

Albufeira is not just a destination; it's an experience, a canvas where you paint your journey with every step. So, embrace the unexpected, for in Albufeira, every day is a new chapter in your travel story. Boa viagem!

6.7 Day 7: Departure or Optional Activities

As the Algarve sun rises on your final day, whether it's a goodbye or just a 'see you later,' let's ensure your last memories are as golden as the sands you've walked on.

Morning Farewell: A Sunrise to Remember

If you're catching an early flight, why not bid farewell with a sunrise stroll along the beach? The Algarve's coastline is at its most peaceful in the early hours. And if you're leaving Faro, the Ria Formosa lagoon greets you with a serene spectacle of light and shadow.

Optional Activity: Dolphin Watching in Lagos

For those with a later departure, seize the day with a dolphin-watching tour. Departing from Lagos Marina, tours start at around €30 per person. With a 4.9-star rating, this experience promises a magical encounter with the ocean's playful inhabitants. Tours typically run from 09:00 to 11:00, but booking in advance and confirming times is best.

Afternoon Adventure: Last-Minute Shopping in Loulé

If your flight isn't until the evening, the market town of Loulé beckons for some last-minute shopping. Open until **14:00**, wander through a crafts, spices, and textiles maze. It's the perfect place to find that unique keepsake. Ask any local for directions – they're always eager to help.

Evening Departure: Sunset at Cape St. Vincent

And for the ultimate finale, if time allows, witness the sunset at Cape St. Vincent, Europe's southwesternmost point. It's a sight that will stay with you long after you've left. The cape's lighthouse stands as a beacon of memories made and adventures yet to come.

Departure Details

When leaving, remember that Faro Airport is just a call away at +351 289 800 800 for any last-minute questions. And if you're traveling by train, the CP (Comboios de Portugal) offers services to Lisbon with departures throughout the day. As you depart, take a piece of the Algarve with you in your heart. Its sunsets, its flavors, and the warmth of its people are now a part of your story. Until next time, adeus!

Chapter 7: Attractions and Activities

7.1 Beaches

Welcome to the sun-kissed shores of the Algarve, where golden sands and azure waters beckon travelers from all corners of the globe. Let's dive into the heart of the Algarve's beach scene, where every grain of sand tells a story of relaxation and adventure.

Praia da Marinha - Lagoa

Nestled along the sun-kissed coast of the Algarve, Praia da Marinha in Lagoa stands as a testament to nature's artistry. This beach, often lauded as one of the globe's most stunning, offers visitors a serene escape with its golden sands and crystal-clear waters. Praia da Marinha is a public treasure with unrestricted access, welcoming visitors to bask in its natural splendor at any hour. The absence of entry fees and fixed operating times means you can enjoy the beach's tranquility from dawn to dusk.

The descent to the beach is an experience in itself. A series of well-maintained steps carve a path through the rugged cliffs, offering panoramic views that rival the beauty of the beach below. As you make your way down, the iconic double-arched rock formation comes into view; its heart shapes a symbol of the enchanting allure of Praia da Marinha. Once on the sand, the beach invites you to unwind under the sun's warm embrace or dip in the inviting waters. The serene ocean offers ideal swimming conditions, while the intriguing rock formations and marine life beckon explorers and snorkelers alike.

The beach's famous 'M' rock, also known as the Cathedral, is a highlight not to be missed. Stroll along the shore to this natural marvel during low tide. From the clifftops, the interplay of rocks creates a heart-shaped frame, offering a unique photo opportunity and a moment to appreciate the wonders of nature. While the beach does not boast extensive facilities, its pristine condition speaks to the careful maintenance it receives. Visitors are encouraged to bring essentials such as sunblock, water, and snacks to ensure a comfortable stay.

Praia da Marinha is accessible by car, with clear signage from Lagoa guiding you along the N125. A parking area is available, followed by a short hike leading to the beach's entrance. Despite its fame, Praia da Marinha often provides a peaceful retreat even during peak season, as it is less crowded compared to other Algarve beaches. This is partly due to its location, which requires a vehicle to reach.

In summary, Praia da Marinha is not just a beach but a destination that captures the essence of the Algarve's breathtaking coastline. It's a place where time slows down, allowing you to savor every moment of your visit to this Portuguese paradise.

Praia de Benagil - Lagoa

Praia de Benagil, a hidden gem in the Algarve's rugged coastline, is a sanctuary of serenity and natural beauty. This intimate beach, embraced by golden cliffs, is a gateway to the Algarve's most breathtaking wonders: the Benagil Sea Cave. The Benagil Sea Cave, known locally as Algar de Benagil, is a majestic sea cave with a unique feature—a circular opening at the top that frames the azure sky. The inside is filled with a gentle, ethereal light from this natural skylight, which gives the space a calm, otherworldly vibe.

Praia de Benagil's soft, golden sand is a welcoming canvas for sunbathers and beachcombers. The beach is relatively small, creating a cozy atmosphere that feels personal and secluded. The nearby cliffs provide wind protection, making it the perfect location for a serene day by the sea. The calm, clear waters of Praia de Benagil are perfect for water sports enthusiasts. Kayaking and paddleboarding are popular activities, allowing visitors to navigate the serene waters and explore the coastline's hidden nooks. For a more relaxed experience, boat tours provide a leisurely way to witness the grandeur of the Benagil Sea Cave up close.

Praia de Benagil is a public beach with no entry fee or set hours, allowing you to visit at your leisure. At the same time, the beach does not offer sunbed rentals; its natural beauty more than compensates. Visitors should bring their beach umbrellas and necessities to enhance their comfort. The journey to Praia de Benagil is straightforward. From the nearby village of Benagil, follow the signs leading you to a designated parking area. From there, a short stroll will take you to the beach's entrance, where the adventure begins.

To fully enjoy the tranquility of Praia de Benagil, it's recommended to visit early in the morning or later in the afternoon, especially during the peak season. This timing allows you to avoid the crowds and have a more intimate experience with nature. Praia de Benagil is not just a destination; it's an experience that captures the heart with its pristine beauty and the promise of adventure. Whether you're there to bask in the sun, explore the sea cave, or simply enjoy the serenity, this beach is a must-visit for any traveler to the Algarve.

Praia de Odeceixe - Odeceixe

Praia de Odeceixe, a picturesque beach located at the confluence of the Seixe River and the Atlantic Ocean, is a slice of coastal heaven in the Algarve region. This beach is distinguished by its unique horseshoe shape, creating a harmonious blend of river and ocean waters that cater to various aquatic pleasures.

Praia de Odeceixe offers the rare opportunity to enjoy both the gentle freshwater of the river and the exhilarating saltwater of the ocean. The river side of the beach, with its warmer and calmer waters, is particularly suitable for families and those seeking a safe swimming environment. In contrast, the ocean side presents the perfect conditions for surfing and bodyboarding, thanks to its robust waves and dynamic currents.

Safety is a priority at Praia de Odeceixe, especially during the bustling summer months. Lifeguards are on duty to ensure a secure experience for all beachgoers, allowing you to relax and enjoy the natural beauty with peace of mind. The local cuisine is an integral part of the Praia de Odeceixe experience. Beachside restaurants serve fresh seafood and traditional Portuguese dishes, providing a gastronomic complement to the day's activities. Reaching Praia de Odeceixe is a breeze. Simply drive to the charming village of Odeceixe and follow the well-marked signs to the beach. Upon arrival, ample parking is available, making it convenient to start your beach adventure.

For those looking to ride the waves, surf schools and rental shops in Odeceixe village offer equipment and lessons for all skill levels. In case you happen to be a seasoned surfer or a beginner, the friendly instructors will help you maximize the beach's surf potential. Beyond the water, Praia de Odeceixe is enveloped by stunning cliffs that provide a dramatic backdrop to the sandy shores. The beach's natural setting is part of the Costa Vicentina Natural Park, a protected area known for its unspoiled landscapes and biodiversity. For the adventurous, the Rota Vicentina trail passes nearby, offering hikers breathtaking views and the chance to explore the region's diverse flora and fauna.

Praia de Odeceixe is more than just a beach; it's a destination that captures the essence of the Algarve's natural charm. It's a place where every visit becomes a cherished memory, in case you're basking in the sun, catching a wave, or simply enjoying the tranquil scenery.

Each beach offers a distinct flavor of the Algarve's diverse coastal landscape. Whether you're here to bask in the sun, surf the waves or just take in the breathtaking scenery, the Algarve's beaches are an endless supply of natural treasures just waiting to be found. So get your sunscreen, grab your hat, and let the Algarve's shores embrace you in warm, sandy arms.

7.2 Historical Sites

The Algarve is not just a picturesque postcard of beaches and resorts; it's a mosaic of history where each stone has a story.

Silves Castle

Silves Castle is a remarkable testament to the area's Moorish past and is nestled atop a hill in the sun-drenched Algarve region. With its robust red sandstone walls and well-preserved structure, it's no wonder that this historic fortress has earned a 4.5/5 rating. Admission is a modest €2.50 for adults, making it an affordable excursion for travelers, and children under ten can explore its storied ramparts free of charge. Daily hours for the castle are 9:00 AM to 5:30 PM, providing ample time to delve into its rich history and enjoy the sweeping views.

History enthusiasts and families will find Silves Castle particularly enchanting. It's the largest castle in the Algarve and one of the most intact examples of Moorish fortifications in Portugal, offering a unique glimpse into the region's Islamic heritage. The castle was originally built by a castro from Lusitania, with subsequent Roman and Visigoth influences. However, during the Moorish occupation, from the 8th to the 13th centuries, the castle flourished, becoming a pivotal stronghold and a symbol of power. The location of Silves Castle, in the historic town of Silves, is easily accessible by car or local bus services, making it a convenient stop for those touring the Algarve.

As you wander through the castle's gates, you're transported back to a time when it was a bustling center of commerce and defense. The architecture is a highlight, with its mix of taipa (traditional mud construction) and Silves sandstone giving the castle its distinctive reddish hue. Inside, the castle houses two cisterns, the Moorish and the Dogs, shrouded in local legends and once vital water sources for the castle's inhabitants. Silves Castle serves as a backdrop for various events throughout the year, including the vibrant Feira Medieval (Medieval Festival) in August, where nightly concerts and spectacles bring the past to life. The castle also hosts sunset concerts, offering a blend of history and culture with a stunning view.

For those looking to immerse themselves further in the experience, the castle's grounds provide panoramic vistas of the old town below and the verdant orange groves that stretch into the countryside. It's a view that has been watched over centuries, from the Moorish era to the present day and continues to captivate all who visit.

In summary, Silves Castle is more than just a historical site; it's a journey through time, offering a rich tapestry of stories, architecture, and panoramic beauty. It is a proud reminder of the Algarve's multifaceted history, waiting to be discovered by curious travelers and history buffs alike.

Lagos' Old Town

Lagos' Old Town, a district steeped in the maritime history of Portugal, is a treasure trove for those drawn to the allure of the past. With a rating of 4/5, it's a testament to its enduring appeal among visitors. Accessibility is a easy, as the Old Town's labyrinth of cobbled streets unfurls just a short walk from the central hotels of Lagos. This proximity invites guests to meander through the historic quarter at their leisure, with no admission fee to hinder their exploration.

The Old Town's picturesque tableau will enchant photographers and cultural enthusiasts. structures with whitewash and vibrant azulejos (ceramic tiles), wrought-iron balconies, and flower-laden terraces offer a feast for the senses and the camera lens.

The Forte da Ponta da Bandeira, a 17th-century fortress, stands guard at the water's edge, its robust walls a silent witness to the town's storied past. Inside, a small museum recounts tales of seafaring adventures and the Age of Discovery, when Lagos was a pivotal launch point for voyages into the unknown.

The ancient walls, remnants of Roman and Moorish fortifications, encircle the Old Town, directing tourists to hidden treasures such as San Antonio and the Church of Santa Maria. The latter is particularly noteworthy for its opulent interior, lavishly decorated with gold from Brazil, reflecting the wealth and power of Portugal's colonial era. For a taste of local life, the Fish Market offers a vibrant atmosphere where the day's catch is displayed in a riot of color and activity. Nearby, the Gil Eanes Square pulses with the energy of street performers and bustling cafés, where one can savor traditional Portuguese pastries or a refreshing glass of vinho verde.

The Old Town is not just a daytime destination; as dusk falls, the area comes alive with a different energy. The sound of Fado music may drift from a nearby tavern, inviting visitors to experience the soulful melodies that are the heartbeat of Portuguese culture. for inquiries or further information. They can provide insights into current events, guided tours, and tips to enhance your visit to this historic enclave.

In essence, Lagos' Old Town is a living museum where every stone tells a story, and every turn reveals a new chapter in Portugal's rich tapestry of history. It's a place to be savored slowly, with eyes wide open and a sense of wonder at the legacy of explorers plus the enduring spirit of discovery.

Chapel of Bones - Faro

In the heart of Faro lies a solemn yet fascinating attraction, the Chapel of Bones. This small chapel, with a rating of 4/5, is a thought-provoking site where the walls are adorned with the skeletal remains of over 1,000 monks. For just €1, visitors can step into a space that encapsulates the fleeting nature of life.

The general public may visit the Chapel of Bones from 10:00 AM to 4:00 PM, except on Sundays when it closes its doors for a day of rest. It's an ideal visit for those with a penchant for the curious and the brave, offering a stark contrast to Faro's sunny beaches and bustling streets. Situated within a short walk from the marina, the chapel is easily accessible and provides a unique detour from the typical tourist path. The

122

contact number for inquiries is +351 289 824 490, where helpful staff can provide more information or assist in planning your visit.

The chapel is part of the larger Carmelite Church of Nossa Senhora do Carmo, an 18th-century baroque masterpiece. Visitors are often struck by the juxtaposition of the church's ornate gold-leafed interior against the starkness of the bone chapel. The entrance to the Chapel of Bones is through the church itself, adding to the experience a sense of discovery as one moves from the grandeur of the church to the contemplative atmosphere of the chapel.

Above the chapel's entrance, an inscription reads: "Pára aqui a considerar que a este estado hás-de chegar," which translates to "Stop here and consider that you will reach this state too." This message invites reflection on the impermanence of life and equality in the face of death. The Chapel of Bones was inaugurated in 1816 and measures four by 6 meters. It was created when cemeteries were often overcrowded, and the exhumation of skeletons was a practical solution to make space for the newly deceased. The bones of the Carmelite friars now form intricate patterns on the walls, serving as a decoration and a memento mori—a reminder of our mortality.

Visiting the Chapel of Bones is a unique experience that leaves a lasting impression. It's a place that challenges visitors to ponder life's deeper meanings and their existence. Whether you're drawn to its historical significance or the profound message it conveys, the Chapel of Bones in Faro is a destination that should not be missed.

Sagres Fortress

Perched on the rugged cliffs of Sagres, the Fortress of Sagres (Fortaleza de Sagres) is a monument of profound historical significance and natural beauty. With a rating of 4.5/5, it's a must-visit for anyone traveling to the Algarve region.

Admission is priced at €3 for adults, with a reduced rate of €1.50 for students and seniors, making it an accessible attraction for all. The fortress operates seasonally, with opening times from 9:30 AM to 5:30 PM during the quieter months of October to March and extended hours until 8:00 PM from April to September to take advantage of the longer days. Ideal for panoramic views and sunset seekers, the fortress offers a breathtaking vantage point over the Atlantic Ocean. It's a location where guests may take in the magnificence of nature's canvas as the sun sets and brilliantly colors the sky. Accessibility is straightforward, with the fortress being reachable by car or bus, ensuring the journey is part of the adventure. For assistance or to learn more about the site, guests should contact the fortress directly at +351 282 620 140.

Prince Henry the Navigator's legacy is inextricably tied to the Fortress of Sagres, who was instrumental in the Portuguese Age of Discoveries. Here, Prince Henry established his famous school of navigators in the 15th century, charting expeditions that would reshape the world. Visitors to the fortress can explore the remnants of this historic site, including the impressive entrance arch and the walls that stretch across the headland, remnants of the original building. The fortress underwent significant renovations in the 1990s, adding modern amenities like multimedia centers, shops, and cafeterias, enhancing the visitor experience.

One of the most striking features within the fortress is the Rosa dos Ventos, a massive circular stone paving believed to have been used for teaching navigation. The site also includes the Church of Our Lady of Grace, originally built in 1570 and restored after the 1755 earthquake that caused widespread destruction in the region.

The Sagres Lighthouse and the A Voz do Mar maze are other highlights, offering unique experiences such as the sound chamber where visitors can listen to the waves breaking against the cliffs. For those interested in the natural world, the fortress is surrounded by the rich flora and fauna of the Southwest Alentejo and Vicentine Coast Natural Park, known for its biodiversity.

In summary, the Fortress of Sagres is not just a historical site; it's a place where the echoes of Portugal's maritime past meet the stunning natural beauty of the present. It's a location that invites contemplation, exploration, and the joy of discovery, making it a jewel in the crown of the Algarve's cultural heritage.

Tips for Travelers:

- **Comfortable Shoes:** Many historical sites have uneven terrain, so wear comfortable footwear.
- **Hydration:** The Algarve sun can be intense, even while exploring shaded ruins, so carry water.
- **Respect the Past:** These sites are precious; treat them with care for future generations to enjoy.

In the Algarve, history isn't just read; it's experienced. Walking through these sites, you're treading the same ground as kings, explorers, and ancient civilizations, each step a journey through time.

7.3 Outdoor Activities

The Algarve's outdoor scene in 2024 is a mosaic of thrilling adventures and serene escapes. Here's a taste of the exhilaration and tranquility that awaits under the Portuguese sun.

XTOURS ALGARVE: Nestled in the heart of Faro, XTOURS ALGARVE beckons the adventurous at heart to delve into the breathtaking beauty of Portugal's southernmost region. With a commitment to showcasing the Algarve's stunning vistas, XTOURS ALGARVE stands out as a premier tourism company, offering an array of outdoor activities designed to connect you with the area's enchanting landscapes.

XTOURS ALGARVE is conveniently situated at Largo de São Pedro 14, Recepção, Faro, 8000-139, making it easily accessible for those staying in or visiting the city. Their doors open wide from 08:00 to 18:00, seven days a week, ensuring that even the busiest travelers can find time to explore. Whether you're seeking the thrill of navigating through hidden caves, longing for the serenity of secluded beaches, or eager to tread along the famed 7 Hanging Valleys Trail, XTOURS ALGARVE has an experience tailored for you. Their Adventure Cave Tour is particularly noteworthy, taking you to the renowned Benagil Cave and more, all while ensuring a stress-free experience with transportation and equipment provided.

To reserve your spot on a tour that promises not just sights but stories, simply reach out to XTOURS ALGARVE at 938 552 571. With no detail overlooked, from safety to enjoyment, each tour is crafted to leave an indelible mark on your memory.

Why Choose XTOURS ALGARVE? Choosing XTOURS ALGARVE means opting for more than just a tour; it's an invitation to immerse yourself in the Algarve's culture and natural splendor. With a deep appreciation for the region's beauty and a passion for outdoor adventure, the team at XTOURS ALGARVE is dedicated to providing experiences that resonate long after the journey ends.

The Algarve region is a tapestry of historical landmarks, pristine beaches, and natural wonders waiting to be discovered. From the bustling city of Faro to the tranquil waters of the Atlantic, every corner of the Algarve tells a story. And with XTOURS ALGARVE, you're not just a spectator but part of the narrative. Embark on a journey with XTOURS ALGARVE, where every path leads to discovery, and every moment is an opportunity to create lasting memories. Book your tour today and experience the Algarve like never before.

Algarve Outdoor Tours: A beacon of adventure on Portugal's sun-kissed southern coast, Algarve Outdoor Tours has been the go-to choice for explorers since 2001. With a flawless 5.0 rating, this esteemed company invites you to unearth the Algarve's most secluded treasures. Operating Hours & Contact Open from 09:00 to 19:00, Algarve Outdoor Tours accommodates the schedules of early birds and sunset seekers alike. To weave your tale of adventure, dial 912 120 123 and secure your place in an upcoming escapade.

The Algarve is a mosaic of rugged landscapes and azure waters, this tour operator offers a diverse palette of activities to experience it all. From the gentle ebb of a kayak on crystal-clear waters to the adrenaline rush of mountain biking down winding trails, there's an activity for every pace and preference. Embrace the ocean's embrace with a Lagos Ocean Kayak tour, where you'll glide past towering cliffs and into yawning caves, including the famed Benagil. Or, opt for a Lagos Kayak Cave Snorkel Trip, merging the tranquility of kayaking with the underwater marvels of snorkeling.

For those who prefer terra firma, the Downhill Scenic Cycling offers a breathtaking descent from the Algarve's highest peaks to its sandy shores, with gravity as your ally. If you're keen on keeping your feet on the ground, the Coastal & Mountain Day Walks will lead you through the region's natural and cultural landmarks.

Why Choose Algarve Outdoor Tours? Selecting Algarve Outdoor Tours means embarking on a journey that's as enriching as it is exhilarating. Their commitment to safety and fun ensures that your adventure is not just about the destination but the stories you'll gather along the way. The Algarve is not just a destination; it's a narrative woven through time, from the historic streets of Faro to the untamed beauty of the Serra de Monchique. With Algarve Outdoor Tours, you become an integral part of this story, one that unfolds with each step, paddle, or pedal.

Join Algarve Outdoor Tours for an authentic encounter with Portugal's beloved southern coast. It's more than a tour; it's an invitation to adventure, a chance to connect with nature, and a journey that promises to captivate your spirit.

GRASPaWASP Tours: Discover the Algarve's allure with GRASPaWASP Tours, a top-rated offering from Algarve Holiday Tours. With a perfect 5.0 rating, they specialize in delivering an exceptional adventure that's thrilling and kind to the environment.

Feel the freedom of the open road in a sleek convertible car. These tours let you soak up the sun and take in panoramic views as you drive along the Algarve's picturesque coastlines and through its charming villages.

Zip through the streets and byways of the Algarve on a classic Vespa scooter. It's an iconic way to easily explore the region's hidden nooks, offering a blend of adventure and culture. GRASPaWASP is committed to eco-friendly tourism. Their vehicles are chosen for their low environmental impact, ensuring your adventure is sustainable.

Available from 09:00 to 19:00, GRASPaWASP Tours provides flexibility for your schedule, enabling you to set off on your adventure whenever it's most convenient for you. Booking your tour is easy—just call 912 979 234. The welcoming staff will assist you in selecting the ideal tour and guarantee that your time will be one to remember.

Embark on a GRASPaWASP tour for a unique and eco-conscious way to experience the beauty of the Algarve.

It's an adventure that promises to be as memorable as it is responsible. Dial now and shift your holiday into high gear!

As you lace up your boots or fasten your life jacket, remember that the Algarve's outdoor activities are not just about the adrenaline rush—connecting with the land, the sea, and yourself.

7.4 Nightlife

The Algarve transforms into a nocturnal wonderland as the sun dips below the horizon. Whether you're a night owl or just want to sip cocktails under the moonlight, the Algarve's nightlife has something for everyone. Let's dive into the rhythm of the night!

Albufeira: Where the Night Comes Alive

The Strip: Albufeira's heartbeat pulses along the famous Strip. This neon-lit stretch is a kaleidoscope of energy, where revelers hop from one bar to another. Hen and stag parties add a splash of mischief, and the air buzzes with laughter. The Strip invites you to dance, sing, and create memories that defy dawn.

Irish Pubs: Albufeira wouldn't be itself without its Irish Pubs. Two favorites stand out:

- **Sherry's Bar**: Small but mighty, Sherry's Bar serves up the best Guinness in town. The staff's warmth makes you feel like family. Start your holiday here, and you'll leave with new friends.

- **33 Sports Bar**: A lively spot for sports enthusiasts, 33 Sports Bar offers cold beers, pool tables, and a vibrant atmosphere. It's where camaraderie meets competition.

Cocktail Magic: For a touch of elegance, head to:

- **Sal Rosa**: The number one cocktail bar in Albufeira, Sal Rosa, offers sea views and Arabic-inspired decor. Sip on world-class cocktails, including their passion fruit sangria—all for just 6 euros.

- **Matt's Bar**: Infamous for wild nights, Matt's Bar is the go-to for hens and stags. Bucking bronco rides, cocktail classes, and boozy brunches—it's a whirlwind of fun.

Vilamoura: Glamour by the Marina

- **Marina Vibes**: Vilamoura's marina is a symphony of luxury yachts and twinkling lights. Stroll along the waterfront, where chic bars beckon. Sip champagne, watch the stars, and feel like a movie star.

- **Black Jack Disco**: For those who love to dance, Black Jack Disco is the place. Open till the wee hours, it's where beats collide with sea breezes. Dress to impress and let the music move you.

Portimão: Riverside Revelry

- **Praia da Rocha**: Portimão's beachfront comes alive at night. Praia da Rocha is a fusion of beach bars, live music, and ocean views. Grab a caipirinha, wiggle your toes in the sand, and sway to the rhythm of the waves.

- **No Solo Água**: This beach club is pure magic. Imagine lounging on plush daybeds, sipping cocktails, and watching the moon dance on the water. No Solo Água is where dreams meet reality.

Faro: A Melodic Farewell

Ria Formosa Views: Faro's Ria Formosa lagoon whispers secrets to night wanderers. Take a sunset boat trip, where the sky blushes pink and the water mirrors the stars. It's a poetic farewell to the Algarve.

Remember: The legal drinking age in Portugal is 18, but many places are lenient. So raise your glass, sway to the music, and let the Algarve's nightlife weave its spell. Cheers to moonlit memories!

Chapter 8: Food and Drink

8.1 Traditional Dishes

The Algarve's culinary landscape is a canvas of flavors, each dish a brushstroke of tradition and innovation. In 2024, the region's gastronomy continues celebrating its roots while embracing the new, offering a feast for the senses as timeless as the Atlantic tides.

Cataplana de Marisco

Dive into the essence of the Algarve with the iconic Cataplana de Marisco. This seafood symphony is served in its namesake copper dish, a testament to the region's maritime heritage. At O Pescador Benagil, rated 4.6 stars, the cataplana bubbles with the day's freshest catch. Prices hover around €30 per person, and the restaurant welcomes diners from 12:00 PM to 10:00 PM. To reserve a spot where the ocean's bounty meets culinary artistry, call +351 282 358 234.

Frango Assado com Piri Piri

No visit to the Algarve is complete without savoring the fiery delight of Frango Assado com Piri Piri. Churrasqueira O Manel in Lagos, a cozy eatery with a 4.3-star rating, has mastered this spicy grilled chicken dish. A meal here is a casual affair, with prices around €15. They're open from 11:00 AM to 11:00 PM, and you can ring them at +351 282 762 791 to ensure you get a taste of this local favorite.

Carne de Porco à Alentejana

For a hearty meal, try the Carne de Porco à Alentejana at Tasca do Viegas. This harmonious blend of pork and clams is a culinary handshake between land and sea. With a 4.4-star rating, Tasca do Viegas serves this comfort food from 12:00 PM to 3:00 PM and 7:00 PM to 10:00 PM. Expect to spend around €20 for a plate full of tradition. Call +351 289 824 739 to book your journey into the Algarve's pastoral past.

Pudim de Laranja

End your culinary adventure on a sweet note with Pudim de Laranja, the Algarve's answer to the orange groves that dot its landscape. At Pastelaria Algarve, rated 4.5 stars, this dessert is a citrusy dream. Open from 7:00 AM to 7:00 PM, a slice of this orange pudding will cost you about €3. Dial +351 289 312 869 to order ahead and savor the sweetness of the south.

Each dish is a story, a melody of flavors that sings of the Algarve's sun, sea, and soil. They're not just meals; they're memories made tangible, served on a plate for you to cherish long after the last bite.

8.2 Best Restaurants

When in the Algarve, dining is not just about satisfying hunger; it's about savoring every flavor, every spice, and every moment. Here's a taste of the best culinary experiences that await you.

Vila Adentro - A Culinary Haven in Faro

Welcome to Vila Adentro, a charming establishment that marries the rich flavors of traditional Portuguese cuisine with contemporary flair. This restaurant is a beacon for food enthusiasts and culture seekers in the picturesque town of Faro.

Features & Offerings:

- **Cuisine:** Indulge in a menu celebrating the sea's bounty with succulent seafood, Mediterranean classics, and European delights. Vegetarian, vegan, and gluten-free alternatives are available to accommodate special dietary demands.
- **Ambiance:** The eatery is located in a historically significant structure with typical azulejos, offering a dining experience steeped in cultural heritage.

- **Ratings:** With a commendable 4.0 rating, Vila Adentro is a testament to its quality and service.

Getting There: Faro is accessible by various modes of transportation. The town is a short drive from Faro International Airport and well-connected by train and bus services. Vila Adentro is conveniently located at PRAÇA DOM AFONSO III, 17, making it an easy find for those wandering the charming streets of Faro's old town.

Contact Details: For those wishing to reserve a spot in this culinary haven, you can contact Vila Adentro at 289 052 173. The restaurant welcomes guests from 12:00 PM to 10:30, ensuring ample time for lunch and dinner explorations.

In summary, Vila Adentro is not just a restaurant; it's a destination that promises an unforgettable journey through the tastes and tales of Portugal. Whether you're a local or a traveler, a meal here will leave you with cherished memories and a longing to return.

O Castelo - Where Gastronomy Meets the Horizon

Perched atop the historic walls of Faro's Old Town, O Castelo presents a dining escapade that rivals the beauty of its panoramic views. With a 3.5 rating, this establishment is a sanctuary for the early birds and the night revelers, operating from 10:30 AM to 2:00 AM.

Features & Offerings:

- **Cuisine:** A diverse menu awaits, featuring a fusion of Bar, Mediterranean, European, and Portuguese dishes, ensuring a treat for every palate.
- **Atmosphere:** The ambiance blends rustic charm and contemporary comfort, making it an ideal spot for a casual brunch or a romantic dinner under the stars.
- **Events:** O Castelo hosts various events, including Fado nights every Monday, live music, and themed parties, perfect for those looking to immerse themselves in the local culture.

Getting There: Faro is well-connected and easily accessible. O Castelo's address is Rua do Castelo 11, Faro, 8000-243, a mere 0.2 km from the heart of Old Town Faro. For those traveling from a distance, the town may also be reached by rail or bus. It is just a short drive from Faro International Airport.

Contact Details: To experience the enchanting evenings or the delightful daytime ambiance of O Castelo, make reservations by calling +351 282 083 518.

In essence, O Castelo is more than a restaurant; it's a destination that promises an experience where every meal is accompanied by an unforgettable view, making it a must-visit for anyone traveling to Faro.

Chefe Branco - A Symphony of Seafood in Faro

At Chefe Branco, the allure of the ocean is brought to the table with each dish crafted to perfection. Located on Rua de Loulé, this Faro favorite is a seafood lover's dream, open daily from 12:00 PM to 11:00 PM and boasting a proud 4.0 rating.

Features & Offerings:

- **Cuisine:** Specializing in Seafood, Mediterranean, European, and Portuguese dishes, Chefe Branco offers a menu that's a testament to the sea's treasures.
- **Special Diets:** Accommodating various dietary needs, the restaurant provides vegetarian-friendly and gluten-free options, ensuring no guest leaves unsatisfied.
- **Atmosphere:** The ambiance blends rustic authenticity and casual elegance, perfect for intimate dinners and lively gatherings.

Accommodation: While Chefe Branco does not offer accommodation, the restaurant is in a locale rich with hotels and guesthouses. Visitors can find comfortable stays within walking distance, with prices typically ranging from €50 to €150 per night for a double room in nearby establishments.

Getting There: Faro is a gem on the southern coast of Portugal, easily reachable by air, land, or sea. Chefe Branco is just 0.6 miles from Old Town Faro, making it a pleasant stroll from most central hotels.

Contact Details: To reserve your culinary voyage at Chefe Branco, please call +351 289 807 584. Whether planning a special occasion or simply seeking the day's freshest catch, Chefe Branco is ready to welcome you.
Embark on a journey where each bite celebrates the sea's bounty at Chefe Branco in Faro.

Mavala Osteria Italiana - Italian Flair

Nestled in the charming streets of Faro, Mavala Osteria Italiana stands as a testament to authentic Italian cuisine. With its doors open from 12:00 PM to 3:00 PM and again from 7:00 PM to 11:00 PM, Tuesday through

Saturday, this culinary gem has earned a flawless 5.0 rating for its impeccable flavors and service.

Features & Offerings:

- **Cuisine:** Delight in a menu brimming with Italian, Mediterranean, and European dishes, including vegetarian, vegan, and gluten-free options to cater to all guests.
- **Ambiance:** Ideal for a romantic supper or a family get-together, the Osteria provides a warm and welcoming atmosphere.
- **Service:** Renowned for its attentive and friendly staff, Mavala ensures a dining experience that feels both luxurious and homely.

Location & Accessibility:

- **Address:** Largo Da Madalena 10, Faro, Algarve, 8000-134.
- **Proximity:** Just 0.3 miles from Old Town Faro, it's a pleasant walk from the city's historic center.
- **Transport:** Easily accessible by local transport, and parking is available nearby for those driving.

Accommodation: While Mavala Osteria Italiana does not offer lodging, Faro has many hotels and guesthouses. Accommodations near the restaurant range from budget-friendly to luxury, with average prices for a double room starting at around €50 per night.

Reservations: To book a table at this slice of Italian paradise, guests can contact Mavala Osteria Italiana at +351 963 100 473. Making reservations in advance is advised, particularly during peak meal times.

In summary, Mavala Osteria Italiana is not just a restaurant; it's an experience that transports you straight to Italy with every bite. Whether you're a local or a traveler, visiting Mavala will surely be a highlight of your time in the Algarve. These are just a few stars in the Algarve's culinary constellation. Each restaurant is a portal to a different world, where the chefs are the narrators, and every dish is a chapter of its own. So, let your palate be the compass that guides you through the Algarve's delicious landscape.

8.3 Local Markets

Vibrant markets come alive in the heart of the Algarve, where the sun-kissed land meets the sea. These bustling hubs are more than just places to shop; they're cultural tapestries woven with the threads of tradition, flavor, and community. Let's explore the Algarve's local markets, where every purchase connects to the region's soul.

Mercado de Loulé: A Feast for the Senses

- **Location**: Loulé, a beautiful traditional Portuguese town with winding streets and a medieval castle.
- **Opening Hours: Daily**

Highlights

- **Arabic-Style Market**: Step into a 120-year-old market hall, its architecture echoing the Algarve's Moorish past.
- **Fresh Produce**: The stalls burst with locally grown fruits and vegetables, from plump tomatoes to fragrant herbs.
- **Fish and Seafood**: Dive into the fish section, where the catch of the day sparkles—perfect for a seafood feast.

- **Cheese and Cured Meats**: Sample artisanal cheeses and savory cured meats, each slice telling a story.
- **Bread and Pastries**: Follow the aroma of freshly baked bread and sweet pastries that melt in your mouth.

Mercado de Olhão: A Seafood Symphony

- **Location**: Olhão, a coastal gem.
- **Opening Hours**: Daily, with a larger market (including a gypsy market) on Saturday mornings.

Highlights:

- **Fish and Seafood Hall**: Wander through the bustling indoor fish market, where the ocean's bounty awaits.
- **Fruit and Vegetable Stalls**: Colorful displays of sun-ripened produce—grab a handful of juicy oranges.
- **Outdoor Area**: Picture-perfect stalls spill onto the streets, offering everything from olives to figs.
- **Local Flavors**: Taste the Algarve's soul in every bite—olive oil, almonds, and fig-based treats.

Mercado Municipal de Portimão: A Culinary Adventure

Location: Portimão.

Highlights:

- **Fish Section**: Dive into the freshest fish and seafood, a symphony of flavors from the Atlantic.
- **Local Vendors**: Meet friendly vendors who share their passion for quality ingredients.
- **Fruit and Veggie Bounty**: Load up on seasonal delights—ripe peaches, plums, and aromatic herbs.
- **Market Buzz**: The lively atmosphere invites you to linger, chat, and discover hidden gems.

Mercado Municipal de Vila de Santo António: Tuna Tales

- **Location**: Vila Real de Santo António.
- **Opening Hours**: 2nd Saturday of the month from 10 am & Every 3rd Sunday (8 am – 1 pm).

Highlights:

- **Fresh Tuna**: Dive into the world of tuna—whole fish and steaks, a local specialty.
- **Fruit and Flowers**: Colorful displays spill onto the cobbled streets, tempting passersby.
- **Community Spirit**: Feel the town's pulse as locals gather to share stories and laughter.

Mercado Municipal de Silves: A Hidden Gem

Location: Silves.

Highlights:
- **Fresh Fruits and Veggies**: A small local market with big flavors—locally grown goodness.
- **Early Mornings**: Arrive early for the freshest picks and maybe even a glimpse of fresh fish.
- **Historic Setting**: The centenary building adds charm to your shopping experience.

In the Algarve's markets, time slows down. Let your senses guide you—touch the sun-warmed tomatoes, inhale the earthy scent of olives, and taste the love that goes into every bite. These markets aren't just about shopping; they're about savoring life, one juicy peach at a time.

Chapter 9: Shopping

9.1 Souvenirs and Local Crafts

As you meander through the Algarve's cobbled streets and vibrant markets, the quest for that perfect souvenir is not just a shopping trip—it's a journey into the heart and soul of this enchanting region.

Mercado de Loulé

Step into the bustling Mercado de Loulé, where the air is rich with the scent of local spices and the chatter of seasoned artisans. Here, you'll find a kaleidoscope of hand-painted Azulejos tiles, each telling its own story of Portuguese culture. Prices for these ceramic treasures start at around €5 for a small piece, making them an affordable and authentic memento.

- **Opening Hours**: Monday to Saturday, 7:00 AM to 3:00 PM.
- **Location**: A short walk from the Loulé town center.
- **Contact**: +351 289 400 600

Porches Pottery

For something truly special, visit Porches Pottery. This studio has been crafting exquisite ceramic ware since 1968. The cost of a gorgeously hand-painted dish or vase might vary from €20 to €100, according on the design's intricacy and size.

- **Opening Hours**: Daily, 10:00 AM to 5:00 PM.
- **Location**: Off the N125 road, near the village of Porches.
- **Contact**: +351 282 352 858

Cork & Co

Don't miss Cork & Co, where the versatile cork oak tree is transformed into everything from sleek handbags to robust wallets. Embrace sustainable fashion with a cork accessory, with prices starting at €10 for smaller items.

- **Opening Hours**: Monday to Saturday, 10:00 AM to 6:00 PM.
- **Location**: Located in the heart of Faro's shopping district.
- **Contact**: +351 289 824 490

Feira de Artesanato de Faro

The Feira de Artesanato de Faro is a treasure trove for those seeking unique handcrafted gifts. The fair showcases the best of Algarve's artisanal talents, from intricate jewelry to hand-woven textiles. Items here range from €15 for smaller crafts to over €50 for elaborate pieces.

- **Opening Hours**: Seasonal; typically open during summer months.
- **Location**: Faro city center, near the marina.

- **Contact**: Information available at local tourist offices.

In the Algarve, every purchase tells a story, every craft speaks of tradition, and every souvenir carries a piece of the region's soul. So, take your time, explore, and let the Algarve's artisans impress you with their timeless creations.

9.2 Shopping Centers and Outlets

Welcome to the sun-kissed Algarve, where shopping is not just a transaction but an experience to savor. Let's dive into the heart of Algarve's retail paradise, where the vibrant culture meets contemporary convenience.

Forum Algarve, Faro Nestled in Faro, is a shopper's haven that mirrors the region's architectural charm. Open daily from 10:00 AM to 11:00 PM, this center boasts a 4-star rating from delighted visitors. To get there, stroll from the city center or hop on a bus that drops you right at its welcoming gates. Need to reach out? Dial 289 889 300 for a friendly chat with their customer service.

Designer Outlet Algarve, Loulé For the fashion-forward, the Designer Outlet Algarve in Loulé is your go-to destination. Imagine strolling through a village-style setting, offering year-round reductions of 30% to 70%. They welcome shoppers from 10:00 AM to 10:00 PM, and with a 4-star rating, they know how to please. Catch a ride from Faro or Vilamoura and be there in no time. Questions? Their number is 289 246 000.

Algarve Shopping, Guia Algarve Shopping in Guia, is an open-air delight, where more than 120 shops await. Rated at 4.2 stars, it's a testament to its quality and ambiance. They're open from 10:00 AM to 11:00 PM, giving you ample time to explore. A short taxi ride from Albufeira will get you there. Jot down 289 105 500 if you need to inquire about a specific store or service.

Each of these shopping centers and outlets offers a unique slice of Algarve life, wrapped in the warmth of Portuguese hospitality. Whether you're hunting for designer deals or local crafts, the Algarve's shopping scene is sure to enchant and entice.

Chapter 10: Practical Information

10.1 Currency and Payments

In the Algarve, the rhythm of commerce beats to the tune of the Euro (EUR), the currency that powers the vibrant markets and quaint shops dotting this coastal utopia. As of 2024, the Euro remains the steadfast medium of exchange, facilitating the seamless purchase of everything from artisanal crafts to indulgent pastries.

Cash or Card? The Algarve embraces both cash and card payments with open arms. While major credit cards are widely accepted, there's a certain charm to carrying a few crisp Euro notes for those small local purchases. ATMs are readily available, particularly in tourist areas, ensuring you're never far from a cash infusion.

Exchange Rates and Tips: Navigating the waters of currency exchange can be smooth sailing with a little local know-how. Avoid airport kiosks and seek out local banks or authorized exchange offices for the best rates. Keep an eye on the current exchange rates to ensure your holiday budget stretches beyond the Algarve's golden beaches.

As you traverse the Algarve's mosaic of experiences, rest assured that the practicalities of currency and payments are as breezy as the region's famed sea winds. With your wallet prepared, every transaction is another step in your Portuguese adventure.

10.2 Local Customs and Etiquette

In the Algarve, local customs and etiquette tapestry is as colorful and intricate as the region's famed azulejos. As you weave through this vibrant cultural landscape in 2024, here are some threads of tradition to guide your journey.

Greetings and Interactions: A warm "Bom dia" (Good morning) or "Boa tarde" (Good afternoon) opens doors and hearts alike. The Algarveans cherish polite exchanges, and a handshake or a light embrace signifies the beginning of any cordial relationship.

Dining Delicacies: When it comes to dining, the Algarve is a feast for the senses. Tipping is customary, with 10% being the norm for exceptional service. Savor the slow pace of meals, especially dinner, which is more than sustenance—a social symphony.

Festive Flair: Embrace the festive spirit by partaking in local celebrations. The New Year's Janeiras—where vocal ensembles serenade the streets with traditional carols—is a musical start to the year. The Sardine Festival in August is a free event where the air is rich with the aroma of grilled sardines, and the nights are alive with music and dance.

Marketplace Manners: In the bustling markets, haggling is an art form. Approach it with a smile, and you'll not only bag a bargain but also a memorable exchange. Remember, it's about the banter as much as the swap.

Beach Etiquette: The Algarve's beaches are pristine, and locals take pride in keeping them that way. Respect the unspoken rule of space—don't plant your umbrella too close to someone else's sandy sanctuary.

Cultural Courtesy: Showing respect is key when visiting historical sites or attending cultural events. Dress appropriately, speak softly, and immerse yourself in the Algarve's rich heritage with reverence.

As you navigate the nuances of the Algarve's local customs and etiquette, you'll find that each interaction is a brushstroke on the canvas of your Portuguese adventure. These moments of connection paint a picture of a journey rich in cultural discovery.

10.3 Useful Phrases in Portuguese

When wandering through the Algarve's sun-kissed landscapes, a few Portuguese phrases tucked in your pocket can open doors to heartfelt encounters and smooth travels. Here's your 2024 guide to speaking like a local, with phrases that will endear you to the Algarvian heart.

Greetings and Essentials

- **Bom dia** (Good morning) - Start your day with this sunny greeting as you enter a pastelaria for a pastel de nata.
- **Boa tarde** (Good afternoon) - Perfect for a friendly nod to the shopkeeper while browsing local crafts.
- **Boa noite** (Good night) - The ideal close to a day, shared with new friends over a glass of vinho verde.

Getting Around

- **Onde fica...?** (Where is...?) - Essential when searching for hidden beach coves or the start of a cliffside trail.
- **Quanto custa um bilhete para...?** (How much is a ticket to...?) - Handy for your bus rides to the next picturesque town.

Dining Out

- **Uma mesa para dois, por favor.** (A table for two, please.) - Set the stage for a romantic dinner under the stars.
- **Posso ver o menu, por favor?** (Can I see the menu, please?) - Begin your culinary adventure with anticipation.

Shopping

- **Quanto custa isto?** (How much is this?) - This question is a must whether you're eyeing ceramic tiles or local honey.
- **Aceita cartão?** (Do you accept cards?) - A practical query in today's cashless society.

Making Connections

- **Como se chama?** (What's your name?) - A personal touch to meeting someone, be it a local artisan or a fellow traveler.
- **Pode me ajudar?** (Can you help me?) - A polite way to request assistance, whether you're lost or just need a recommendation.

Emergencies

- **Preciso de ajuda.** (I need help.) - For those unexpected moments, this phrase is a lifeline.

- **Onde fica o hospital mais próximo?** (Where is the nearest hospital?) - Vital information that you'll hopefully never need.

Farewells

- **Foi um prazer conhecer-te.** (It was a pleasure to meet you.) - Leave a warm impression as you bid farewell to your Algarve acquaintances.
- **Até a próxima!** (Until next time!) - Because once you've experienced the Algarve, you'll surely want to return.

These phrases are more than mere words; they're keys to unlocking the true essence of the Algarve. They reflect an eagerness to embrace the local culture and a readiness to experience all the beauty this coastal paradise offers. So speak a little Portuguese, and watch the Algarve smile back at you.

Conclusion

As our journey through the Algarve Travel Guide comes to a close, we reflect on a region that is more than just a destination; it's a vibrant tapestry woven with the threads of history, culture, and natural beauty. The Algarve is not just a place you visit; it's a world you experience.

Every element of the Algarve tells a story, from the golden cliffs that embrace the Atlantic to the tranquil hills that roll in the hinterland. It's a story of fishermen who dance with the tides, chefs who conjure magic with simple ingredients, and towns that hold secrets of the ages in their cobbled streets.

The Final Word on Costs: The Algarve remains one of Europe's most value-packed destinations. Whether you're sipping a €2 coffee in a seaside café or indulging in a gourmet dinner for €30 at a top-rated restaurant, you'll find that your euros stretch far here.

Ratings and Reviews: With an average rating of 4.5 across its accommodations, restaurants, and attractions, the Algarve consistently delights travelers. It's a testament to the region's commitment to excellence and the warm hospitality of its people.

Getting There and Around: Accessibility is the Algarve's middle name. Faro International Airport is a gateway and a network of buses and trains connecting every corner, so you're never far from your next adventure.

Contacts to Remember: Keep the Algarve Tourism Board number (+351 289 800 400) handy for any assistance, and remember, the locals are just as helpful, always ready to share their slice of paradise with a smile.
In the Algarve, every sunset marks the end of another beautiful chapter, and every dawn ushers in the promise of discoveries. So, as you turn the last page of this guide, remember that the Algarve isn't just a place you've read about—it's a living, breathing experience waiting to welcome you.

Until we meet on these sunlit shores, we leave you with a heartfelt 'até breve' (see you soon) and the assurance that the Algarve will always have a new story to share each time you return.

Printed in Great Britain
by Amazon